782463

Greatbatch
Boundary Hunter

Greatbatch
Boundary Hunter

An autobiography with
James Harding

Hodder Moa Beckett

ISBN 1-86958-429-5

© 1996 Mark Greatbatch

Published in 1996 by Hodder Moa Beckett Publishers Limited
[a member of the Hodder Headline Group]
4 Whetu Place, Mairangi Bay, Auckland, New Zealand

Typesetting and editorial services by Gil Dymock, Kaiwaka

Printed by Wright & Carman (NZ) Limited, Wellington

All rights reserved. No part of this publication may be reproduced or transmitted in any form or by any means, electronic, mechanical, including photocopying, recording or any information storage and retrieval system, without permisssion in writing from the publisher.

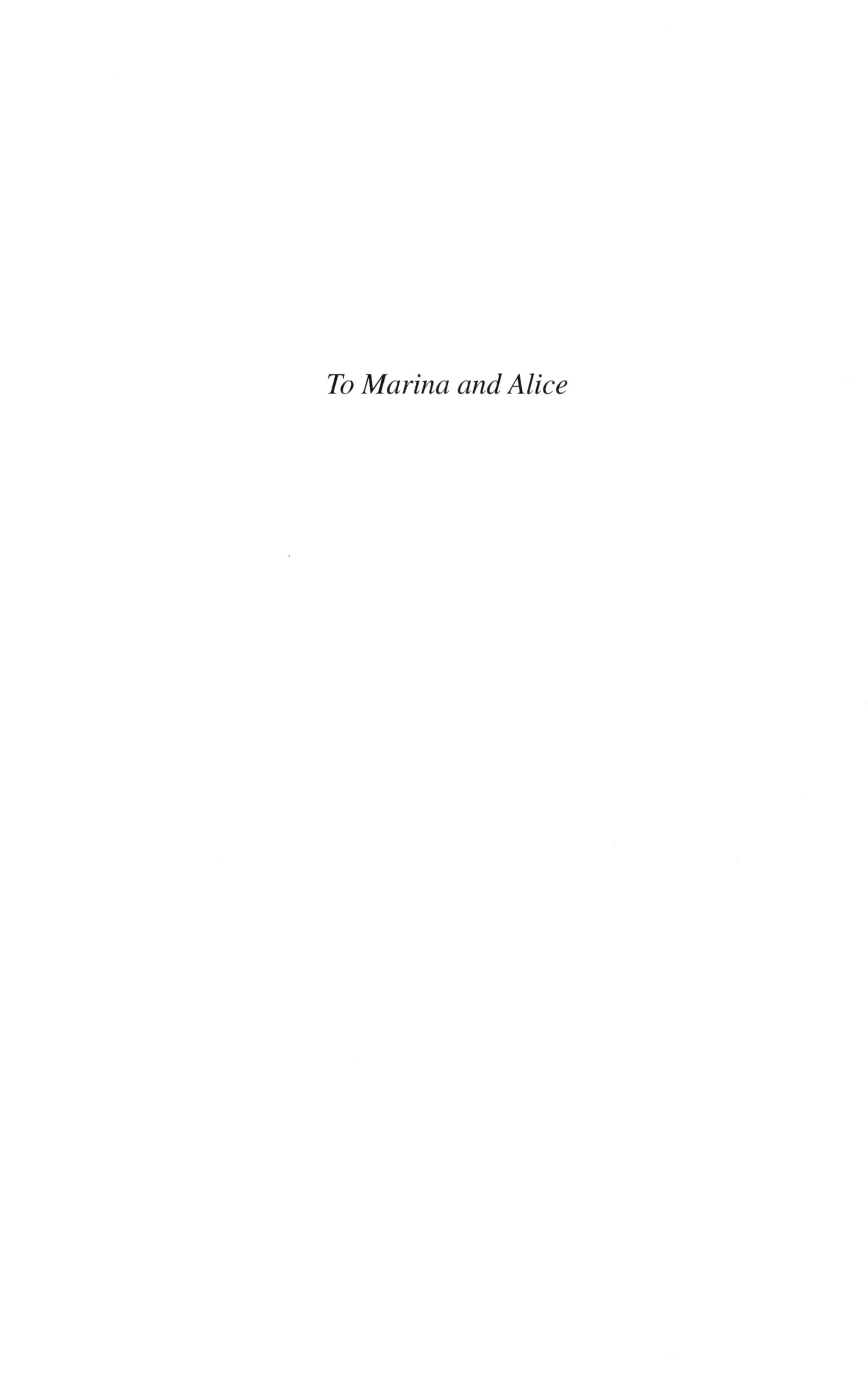

To Marina and Alice

Mark Greatbatch will go down in history as one of the men who turned cricket into a highly entertaining spectator sport for not only New Zealand fans, young and old, but all cricket followers around the world.

When Mark walks out to the wicket, anticipation rises as everyone knows that something is about to happen. Heartbeats will quicken and excitement soar as Mark starts dispatching the ball around the ground in his cavalier style – the style that New Zealanders love to watch.

We at PONY are honoured to be involved with Mark and the publication of his book, and are very proud to sponsor him and have him promoting our products.

Read and enjoy this book, which will give everyone an insight, not only into the big-hitting batsman, but also the man beneath the helmet.

GRANT WYATT
Managing Director

GLOSSARY

Nicknames and abbreviated names

Nathan Astle	Nathe
John Bracewell	Braces
Ewen Chatfield	Chats
Jeff Crowe	Chopper
Martin Crowe	Hogan
Stephen Fleming	Flem
Trevor Franklin	Franko
Mark Greatbatch	Paddy
Richard Hadlee	Paddles
Chris Harris	Harry
Mark Haslam	Has
Andrew Jones	Jed
Chris Kuggeleijn	Kuggs
Rod Latham	Roc
Warren Lees	Wally
Dipak Patel	Dipper
Mark Plummer	Plums
Blair Pocock	Pokey
Ken Rutherford	Ruds
Martin Snedden	Sneds
Ian Smith	Stockley
John Wright	Shake

CONTENTS

FOREWORD

by John Wright

Mark Greatbatch is a cricketer who has experienced some unbelievable highs and some real lows and I've been in the dressing room with him on many of those occasions. The lows have puzzled me – I could never work out why a player of his quality would be left out of a side, nor did I believe any run of poor form would continue, provided he was batting in the right spot, sticking to the basics and playing in the right environment. The highs have been a joy to share and it's been great to see a player who enjoys the success of others so much achieve outstandingly himself.

I was coaching a Northern Districts under-20 side when I first came across Paddy; this thickset, blond eighteen-year-old playing for the Aucks at University Oval – full of confidence, maybe even brashness at times, and definitely with a healthy dose of natural ability. The things that stood out were his ambition, will to win and demonstrable enjoyment of the game . . . not to mention his ready response to anything that was thrown at him!

Paddy played his first test against England and was in with me when I picked up a hundred. Always the extrovert, he started hammering my back in congratulations . . . to the point where I had to ask him to ease up – I'm glad I didn't have to play footy against him! His second-innings hundred was most notable for its maturity. Here was a guy playing in his first test handling a heap of pressure and some very accurate spin bowling from Emburey as if he'd been doing it for years.

In India in 1988 I saw the selfless side of Paddy Greatbatch on two occasions. In the game between the first two tests, Kuggs and Blainy scored hundreds while Paddy, for the fifth consecutive time, couldn't reach 20. Despite his disappointment, he was the first guy to get out and applaud the centurions off the field – a classy gesture for a determined young guy who may well have been in danger of losing his test spot. As it happened, Paddy did come right and during the third test, in the midst of a great partnership with Stockley, made it through to the last over before stumps. The first ball of the over was on his legs and he tickled it fine for a regulation single, but his concern for team and teammates came first and he stayed where he was to play out the final over himself. Most batsmen, myself included, would have been off like a shot.

Perth, of course, has been his greatest triumph to date and remains the greatest innings I have seen in terms of value to a team. Had he been dismissed, we would have been beaten – it's that simple. It was Paddy at his best; fantastic balance, weight slightly forward and terrific composure in the face of the Australian onslaught. The Aussies are always tough critics but he has been rated over there ever since.

In the field he's been great; always fizzing and often pulling off the spectacular. I would have to say, just quietly, that on occasion Paddy has a knack of making the comfortable ones look like miracle catches! I enjoyed leading him and felt he was an easy guy to manage, provided I was straight with him and stressed commitment and team loyalty; two things on which he put great emphasis. In my time he was an automatic choice, he was a competitor and he was very proud to play for New Zealand.

It's ironic, but I think some of Paddy's problems have come from his amazing batting in the 1992 World Cup, when the boys on the terraces were reluctant to get another beer for fear of missing another massive blow. For a while after he seemed to suffer from a form of cricketing schizophrenia, swapping personalities from the gutsy crease occupier to the adrenalin-pumped boundary junkie. For my money, he's always been a middle-order player in the longer game and still has a heap to offer the New Zealand side.

When the environment is right and the team are working hard for each other, there's a fair chance that Paddy Greatbatch will be at his best – a fine batsman, a great competitor and a guy who demanded the best of himself every time he strapped the pads on.

INTRODUCTION

by James Harding

I first met Mark Greatbatch at intermediate school – even then he had a big reputation. While most of the positions in the school batting order were open for debate, Mark Greatbatch would open the batting, and he would keep wicket . . . end of story. Batch was a big kid and could hit it a long way, although the meagre dimensions of Cornwall Park No 3 meant the hits are probably bigger in the memory than in reality.

Many adults who came across the young Greatbatch will probably remember a young man with scant regard for authority. If this is so I believe they do him an injustice. Sure, Mark Greatbatch wasn't an automatic follower of rules, but he always had his role models and mentors and respected well placed authority more than that assumed by age.

Auckland Grammar School was pivotal in the development of Batch and like many youngsters he set his sights on playing top level sport for the school. Some teachers struggled with the boisterous and often feisty young man but men like John Graham, Dave Syms and Steve Cole knew how to get the best out of his prodigious talent.

John Graham once remarked that Mark Greatbatch was more conscientious than most about the responsibility of maintaining the school's tradition of sporting success, and he contributed to that tradition in two codes. As a cricketer, selection for the First XI was a fait accompli but he had to work hard to make the First XV. The 1981 side won the championship after some early hiccups and Batch played some magic footy, eventually being picked for the New Zealand Secondary Schools side which, disappointingly, didn't take the field.

It was through his rugby connection that the nickname "Paddy" was coined. As a young man of 15, he was heavy enough to play open grade, and wisely decided the wing was the safest spot. At the time Paddy Batch was playing test rugby on the wing for Australia so the connection was obvious.

There are those who think the nickname came from the mode of transport by which he was escorted into town after an impromptu exit from Eden Park, but that came much later!

Mark Greatbatch has an army of friends and supporters largely because he has managed to resist the seduction of fame. In a country where a reasonable knock in a one-dayer will put your name in lights, Paddy has remained consistent in his dealings with his friends and with members of the public. He has been the man of the moment on a number of occasions but has never been too busy to chat with supporters or have a couple of quiets with his mates.

The high points in the Greatbatch career have been matched by nearly as many disappointments, but he has faced misfortune with dignity, has worked hard and been reselected time and time again. On many occasions his omission has been mysterious, particularly when, Martin Crowe aside, he is one of the few players people will pay the price of admission to come and see.

Certainly, entertainment value is not an international cricketer's primary selection criterion but his frequent re-calls would make the supposition that there have been a lack of adequate replacements self-evident.

Mark Greatbatch is a big-hearted individual and whether visiting primary schools or signing autographs after games is always generous with his time. He has a great appetite for the rewards that success brings but his life with Marina and wee Alice in their lovely home in Hawke's Bay provides a perfect escape from the public demands. To his friends and supporters Mark Greatbatch has nothing to prove – he has given us hours of pleasure as a cricketer and has been totally reliable as a friend.

Reselection for the tour of Pakistan in 1996 may demand more is written on the career of Mark Greatbatch – *Boundary Hunter* is the story so far . . .

Perth

Watch the ball! After 655 minutes of batting such a reminder should be unnecessary, should become redundant. It's not, and it doesn't. At Perth in late 1989 I turned it into a mantra, made it part of a routine I followed for 485 balls. This strict discipline kept me going and helped break down a massive task into manageable pieces. In the end it led to a rescued test match and some records which would tag me as marginally more attractive to watch than synchronised swimming.

When I look back and think that I scored at an average rate of around 13 runs per hour it was little wonder the clicking of turnstiles was not going to deafen anyone during that game. Walking off the WACA with Martin Snedden, the job done, the Aussies fuming, a biggish hundred to my name and a match saved from almost certain defeat, scoring rates were the last thing on my mind. Not surprisingly, a beer was high on the list but I really just wanted to get to the dressing room, put my feet up and enjoy the moment with the teammates who had worked so hard off the field to keep us going in the middle.

Cricket must be one of the few games where a draw gives rise to satisfaction and the feeling of real accomplishment. The dressing room mood was one of celebration and filled with all the back-slapping and frothiness that goes with it. I wandered into the room, sat down in the corner that had been my lair and flopped over on my side, not so much physically tired but mentally pretty much spent.

It was a superb feeling to have the respect of cricket's toughest competitors and I felt privileged to share a drink and talk cricket with the likes of Border and Simpson, tapping into their vast store of cricketing knowledge. That I would be sitting in that room in those circumstances would have attracted long odds at any time on that tour as there was little to suggest glory in any form from our early performances.

We arrived at Perth having had the sort of preparation which wouldn't have prepared us for an exhibition game let alone matches against two state sides and a test with an Australian team which had just streeted England in the Ashes series. Finding Perth-like conditions in New Zealand just isn't going to happen. A couple of club games in Hastings and a hastily arranged open wicket on the No 2 at Lancaster Park and we were off! The Lancaster Park track was a dirty green seamer – one of those square 'em up and rap 'em on the inside thigh types – so although we'd all had a bat and a bowl there was nothing to suggest test match readiness about us. I'm not saying we were totally underdone when we arrived in Perth but I can't help but feel that if we were a piece of scotch fillet we'd have been sent back.

The other missing ingredient in this Mission Impossible was the great fast bowler. Richard Hadlee had declared himself unavailable because of his dodgy achilles tendon – a withdrawal similar to the All Blacks of the time competing without Foxy. Paddles and Hogan were our only genuine matchwinners and to lose one of them pointed to a hard road ahead.

We arrived at Perth for a one-dayer and a four-dayer

against Western Australia. I had heard the Australian national side were no strangers to a bit of lip on the field but these guys were in a class of their own. Class is probably the wrong word as the repartee was more the sort of material you would find on a Rodney Rude tape – subtlety was not their long suit. A look at the scorecards begs the question 'how the hell would you know, Greatbatch!' as I managed to scrape together 6, 0 and 3 in my time at the crease. I know because they didn't wait to see if you were going to be a threat before they ripped into you.

More recently I have been known to have a wee word back in the face of sledging but when you're a relative newcomer and it's zinging round your ears on a bouncy one, focusing on the task at hand is the way to go.

We were stuffed out of sight in the one-dayer with Tom Moody – another of those superb Australian players who can't establish themselves in the top side – scoring a rapid 94 to pass us with ease. In the four-dayer, only a staunch Wrighty special and some hi-jinks from Stockley rescued us from what could have been an embarrassing loss.

The match against South Australia produced the almost standard M.D. Crowe century at the Adelaide Oval and it was nice for Chopper to pick up a ton against his old state, made better by the fact that his former teammate David Hookes was still lining up for them. My search for form remained elusive, although I got myself to 30-odd before being hit in the balls, which dulled more than my enthusiasm. I got through to stumps but was out the next morning and really felt short of time in the middle with the test just days away.

The presence of one Brendon 'the Bro' Bracewell set me on the path to some form. The practice facilities at the Adelaide Oval are outstanding and the Bro was keen on a bowl so I jumped at the chance to have as many nets as possible before the test. Having a net at some grounds is often valueless as the bounce is inconsistent and the ball behaves unusually – you wouldn't find many players eager for a net at some of our grounds. At Adelaide, though, the practice strips were on a par with what was out in the middle and having a quality bowler like the Bro charging in and bowling competitively (do the Bracewells know another way?) gave me a good workout and the chance to start hitting it in the middle again.

More importantly, I began to *feel* confident and my lack of runs was not hanging over me as we approached Perth. Much the same way as a goalkicker will have a few kicks at practice and be more concerned with how he's striking it than whether the kicks are going over, I was approaching Perth feeling good about my game and keen to experience a test match against the side which, year in and year out, are the toughest competitors in world cricket.

I was interviewed before the game and conveyed a positive approach about playing at the WACA, not easy when your form doesn't warrant such comments. I think it underlines further the way I was feeling – that the past was the past and had no bearing on what was to unfold.

Danny Morrison was interviewed at the same time and remarked that we had our backs against the wall – an interesting comment given that a ball hadn't been bowled! I think, though, that Danny was being more realistic than pessimistic as we had not only lost Paddles but Andrew Jones had cracked a finger in the state match and John Bracewell had picked up a similar injury in the nets prior to the test. Three of our most experienced players out was something of a disaster but it did help to get us together as sporting teams tend to in difficult circumstances.

My regard for the Aussie practice facilities increased as the Bro continued to charge in and the Perth nets were every bit as good as Adelaide's.

By coin-toss I was ready and couldn't wait to get amongst it. Wrighty had other ideas and a hint of green on the track meant we fielded. I have always been keen on giving it plenty in the field as it is easy for the game to drift if you're not involved and there is no noise or encouragement about.

Wrighty pulled in a screamer early on to get rid of Taylor but from then on it was a leather hunt with David Boon savaging 200. It is another of cricket's ironies that Boonie's superb double-century has been consigned to a footnote whenever the test is discussed. His was an innings of far greater majesty and dominance than mine and his cutting in particular is fresh in my memory – there weren't too many queuing up for a spell in the gully that day and Wrighty at times was in danger of injury.

Sneds and Danny toiled away for two days and picked up four wickets each with my only contribution a diving catch to get rid of Steve Waugh. Batting against scores of 500-plus is always difficult because winning is almost certainly out of the question and your targets are things like the follow-on rather than the opposition score. On the upside, it does narrow your focus. However, losing three key players and having the opposition score 500 meant that we had had enough of galvanising experiences and were looking forward to being dealt a couple of reasonable hands over the three remaining days.

We made it through to stumps OK but early the next morning Vance was bowled by a perfect Terry Alderman outswinger which neatly plucked out his off stump. I'd had a swim early that morning and a good net (more full-on stuff from the Bro), a routine I was to repeat for the remainder of the match. I was striking it well from the start and although the bounce took some getting used to I was getting into line and well forward, which was critical. Batting with Hogan is always enjoyable and we seemed to be cruising at 173-2 before I flicked at a widish one from big Merv and that was that. Hogan followed soon after and the follow-on rapidly materialised as none of the remaining batsmen could get a start. I was disappointed to get out when I did but felt that I was back in nick and ready for another crack at them.

Not so eager that I wanted a bat before lunch but there

I was replacing the skipper who guided one to third slip where Border took it expertly. As if setting the tone for what was to come I cut and drove my way to nought in 39 minutes and Bert Vance and I put on nought for the second wicket in 27 minutes. The tone had been set and we luncheoned uneasily at 21-2.

Although slow, I was not concerned – I was playing to the conditions really – because we obviously needed to be low risk and we were up against some very accurate and quite rapid bowling. I actually left one which bounced over middle, testimony to the nature and quality of the bounce but also to the confidence with which I was leaving the ball. It sounds like an unusual thing to be proud of, and you certainly don't hear people in the bar talking about 'glorious leaves', but knowing where your sticks are is vital, particularly when you're in defensive mode and looking to play as few deliveries as possible when the ball is new.

The Aussies were pretty keen to check out of their hotel but I felt if Hogan and I could stick in for a while the test could definitely be saved. The pitch was quickish but not 'skiddy quick' and the ball was coming through nicely, generally still rising when it went past – the slips were certainly a long way back. Steve Waugh must have got a sore throat in the gully because he was a distance away and I could hear him quite clearly!

Unfortunately, Hogan nicked one off Moody who picked up a very tidy scalp for his first in test matches. Although he was considered a part-timer, Moody's 6ft 8in made him awkward and the ball that got Hogan was a jaffa, seaming away and taking the edge. Dipak Patel stuck it out for about an hour and importantly got us through to tea before getting an lbw decision of doubtful accuracy. Chopper came in and as usual displayed his incredibly laid-back style. Outwardly he gave the impression that he was having a hit in a club game and his demeanour helped to deflect the enormity of the task. Stumps was the goal and thanks to Chopper picking up a few boundaries off Border toward the end of the day we finished in reasonable shape at 168-4. In our second innings we had lost two wickets in the first session but only one in each of the subsequent sessions. Although not big partnerships in run-scoring terms, they all occupied valuable time and at least gave us a fighting chance going into day five.

I've mentioned that routine was important throughout this innings and I followed a routine off the field as well. Every night the team would meet at an Irish bar across the road from the hotel and have a beer together. As a former resident of Perth and not in the playing eleven, Brendon Bracewell would follow a different sort of routine which involved him kicking on until late at night most nights of the test. Late night or not, he was always first to training and last to leave and was a constant source of encouragement throughout.

On the morning of the final day I had my morning swim and an early breakfast and then headed to the ground for a net and the chance to shower and rest before the start of play. With twenty minutes to go I reached for my batting trousers only to discover they were back at the hotel and not retrievable before the start of play.

In a panic I canvassed the troops, searching for some adequate replacements, and the first and only volunteer was one J.G. Bracewell. It was a lovely gesture from Braces but you don't need a degree in Human Anatomy to recognise that the lean Bracewell's strides were not going to sit comfortably over my more considerable gluteal parameters. It would have been like Stockley lending a pair of his to Trevor Franklin. But beggars can't be choosers, so I donned the offering and spent the first session adjusting my box, tugging at my strides and trying to avoid a savage dose of chafing. Looking for all the world like a stand-in for Barry Gibb in the Staying Alive video, I was a relieved man to come in at lunch to see my favourite pair had been retrieved from the hotel.

Chopper and I began the morning session conscious

that the new ball was just a few overs away. That was to be the first of many mini-goals I would set throughout the day. As the last of the specialist batsmen, we knew that seeing the new ball off was very much our responsibility and Border surprised neither of us by grabbing it as soon as it was due. What did surprise me was that he gave it to Lawson, who I found a lot more comfortable than either Hughes or Rackemann.

We were just getting set and re-establishing ourselves when Chopper played back to Hughes and was leg before. Stockley got a difficult one next ball which he steered to slip and it was over to a very young and nervous Chris Cairns to face the hattrick from the snarling Hughes. The confident competitor of today is in stark contrast to the jittery young man who wandered onto the WACA that afternoon.

Although it may have appeared the beginning of the end to some, I was still confident we could save the game. It was an excellent wicket and I had no doubts about my ability to stay there. A bit edgy he may have been, but Chris Cairns was an accomplished batsmen who could stick around if he needed to. Of course, the fall of two wickets set the Aussies buzzing and the peace was replaced with a steady stream of advice, abuse and frequent reminders of the score. Merv had been lifted another notch and was really difficult, always at you and trying new ways to get you out. He wasn't short of a word either but I preferred that to what flew out from under the Zapata a few years later at Eden Park!

Cairns played well to get us to lunch and it was satisfying to get through the session after losing Chopper and Stockley so rapidly. The mood in the dressing room was changing, for although we still had plenty to do the guys could sense that the task wasn't totally beyond us and another session like the last one might just give us a shot. I continued the routine of showering and changing into fresh kit and returned the Bracewell strides with gratitude!

I wasn't particularly impressed with the umpiring in this game and Cairns' dismissal shortly after lunch was unfortunate not only for him but also for our hopes of saving the game. Cairnsy had played well and to score 28 in ninety minutes was a superb effort. The faint upside was the appearance at the crease of Martin Snedden, who I knew would sell his wicket dearly. The other thing about Sneds is his calmness and common sense, a big help when you're looking for every opportunity to think of ways of keeping yourself going and staying focused.

I had a really long period in the nineties and I'd be lying if I said I never thought about my hundred. One thing that helped was my slowness throughout; when you're scoring thirteen runs an hour, being on 90 meant a hundred was some time away.

When Rackemann came loping in for the umpteenth time any punter worth his salt would have wagered heavily on me standing up, taking it on the splice and pushing it down the wicket. Talk about give you nothing, he actually conceded less runs than overs bowled in the second innings. This delivery was different though, a little fuller, and I pushed it past mid-on for two and after 465 minutes and 341 balls I had three figures against Australia. I'd like to think I knuckled straight back down to the job but next ball I survived a huge lbw shout after an indifferent defensive push and then I pushed one to Steve Waugh at mid-off and he nearly threw me out at the bowler's end – frenetic stuff in the context of the game!

Sneds came down at the end of the over and said something like 'well played – but hey let's finish this'. As usual he was right on the mark and by now we had a new target, namely knocking off the deficit. It was important to have something different to think about as time targets have their place but batting is about scoring runs and the new focus came just at the right time. The Aussies were starting to realise that their altered travel plans were going to have to be reviewed and Allan Border was beginning to demonstrate why he was frequently referred to as 'Grumpy'. There were a few problems with the ball just before tea and although sometimes these things can affect your flow I was happy to chat with Sneds as valuable minutes were used up.

The contrast in the dressing room between tea on day four and tea on day five was dramatic. The boys were doing anything to keep us going and as Ian Smith was to comment later 'we fought every ball with them'. After such a long struggle the target was in reach but, with respect to Danny and Willie, an early wicket in the final session would probably be sufficient to lose the game. Danny's lack of nick was evident in the first innings when he leant forward and pushed one into the covers – off his helmet!

A look at the scorecard would reveal a draw but not the tension of the final session. We knew that ninety minutes' batting would be enough but we still kept our targets short term – ball by ball, over by over.

With six runs to go before we cleared the deficit, Sneds pushed one from Alderman to Boon who grabbed it on the half volley. I thought he had indicated early that he hadn't caught it but the umpires conferred and Border was in pushing hard. I wandered down and suggested there must be some doubt, to which Border's reply was that I bugger off and let the umpires do their job – rather strange given his frequent advice to them. At that stage he had played exactly 100 tests more than I had, so I guess he felt I had some time to serve. Thankfully, the umpires made the right call and on we went.

This incident brought out the first words from Boon in eleven hours in the field. Often short leg will have an occasional word but Boonie just crouched there silently, ball after ball. If Steve Waugh had been standing there for eleven hours I would have gone deaf!

Two runs later I nicked Lawson (who up until then had not been particularly troublesome) passed a tired Alderman at slip and began an unhappy last spell for the big fast bowler. Next ball I glanced to leg and strolled down the pitch for one, not noticing that I was on a collision course with him. Inevitably I cannoned into him and the toys went everywhere. Ian Chappell commented on Channel 9 that 'he would back the fifteen stone ex rugby union player if it got physical' but I was actually turning around to make a gesture of apology when the stream of abuse poured out. If anything, I just tried harder.

A glide from Alderman meant Australia were batting again, which meant we could rearrange our timing less ten minutes. Sneds had been batting for two hours, which is a heck of a long time for a tailender. We knew that Rackemann and Hughes would be back for one last spell and, as they had been throughout the match, would be the most difficult to keep out. Terry Alderman is a bowler of the highest class but he wasn't going to do us for pace and as left handers we automatically nullified his most potent weapon, the late outswing to the right hander. Lawson seemed out of sorts but managed to find the edge of both our bats only to see Alderman shell us both.

At eight runs ahead with an hour to play the Mervaerobics began. This was it – we weren't far enough in credit to consider the game safe and the Aussies knew this was their last chance. I was starting to tire mentally but knew I had to stick in to shield the tail. Sneds was absolutely peppered and had some interesting souvenirs on his body after the Hughes onslaught. There was no thought of me farming the strike but it was pretty tempting during that little working over.

The drinks trolley rolled out one more time and there was the Bro bringing out some new gloves and a healthy dose of encouragement. 'Going well Batchy – one more hour mate.' By now my gloves were never quite dry, but the bat was feeling good in my hands Once I shot off and changed gloves without asking the opposition captain, the usual courtesy – I had the feeling such a request might have just made him more grumpy!

Getting through plenty of deep breathing and dancing on my toes, I was also making sure we didn't face any more balls than was absolutely fair. I felt very pumped up and my delight at Sneds nicking one past Alderman was almost audible. It was 5.30 when I first thought we were there but Border had given no indication that he'd had enough. Rackemann pitched one up for about the fourth time in eleven hours and I hammered it down the track sure that my 150 was up – incredibly he got down to it and parried it away. I was conscious of bringing up my 150 but there was no way I was getting out so the big shots stayed in the bag. As it happened I didn't add another run and within five minutes Border was strolling over to the umpires.

Filled with feelings of relief and immense pride, it was great to shake hands with the Aussies knowing that their best wasn't good enough – for this match anyway. I was determined that Sneds and I would walk off together as his innings was as crucial as mine. Coming as it did from a guy who in terms of technique shouldn't have lasted thirty minutes let alone three hours against that sort of attack, Sneds' knock proved that brains and guts are more than ample substitutes for technical proficiency. In his match preview that morning, Jerry Coney had likened our chances of saving the test to the chances of Canada beating the All Blacks – tenner on Canada thanks Mantis.

I must have sat there with my gear on for an hour just soaking it in. It was a thrill to get a call from Mum, congratulating me and checking on how I was, and I was looking forward to a beer with Dad, who had made the trip to Perth – money well spent Owie!

I wandered into the Australian dressing room and was greeted by the sight of the two most difficult bowlers, Rackemann and Hughes, caked in ice from virtually the hip down. I wanted to grin but felt a measure of sympathy when I saw Rackemann's toes, red and bleeding. It was great chatting with the Aussies and then, being faithful to the routine of the match, it was in to the Irish bar for a few quiets. Perth's Kiwis were there in force and gave a huge roar when we strolled in, which was a bit embarrassing really, but we soon got immersed in the spirit and had a fantastic night.

When the phone rang at 7am I was revising my opinion of the night before! Interviews with the media, down to Fremantle to catch up with Andy Taylor and the F&P crew in the Whitbread and then we were on the plane home, accompanied all the way by some fine representatives from the Shiraz stable.

I was interviewed when I got off the plane and the combination of very little sleep and a persistent Shiraz made me feel that it was prudent to leave my sunglasses on. Looking like Michael Jackson (although he's a bit whiter), I mumbled my way through a few responses and was on my way home. Perth was over, a proud memory and a unique moment in my cricketing life. Within a few days I was out in the middle again and after an hour or so defending on a green one at Eden Park my partner at Perth had me out caught behind. I was back down to earth with a thud. Thanks Sneds.

Getting a Start

I guess every kid starts in the backyard, playing heroic knocks in partnership with the stars of the day or picking up a hattrick against Australia to win a one-dayer. The Greatbatches were no different and we even had a net and a roller for our makeshift pitch. As a younger brother I recall getting the lion's share of the rolling duties but as my brother was a "nasty fasty" and five years my senior there was considerable self-interest in preparing a reliable surface. My dad had played a bit of cricket and brother Paul was dead keen so we had many hours out the back in fierce competition.

Growing up in the Auckland suburb of New Lynn makes me a "Westie", a group not known for a deep fascination with the arts of cricket. Come to think of it, it was hard to concentrate with all those V8s chugging away in the background.

After I'd gained some early education at St Mary's in New Lynn the family moved to Epsom, where Mum had bought a rest home. Unfortunately, there was no provision for a cricket pitch so Paul and I had to construct our own mini-oval, which involved re-arranging the clothesline and jamming into a narrow area where there was little or no room to escape the Paul Greatbatch thunderbolts. I knew I was in trouble when his run up grew longer and longer and eventually started out on Epsom Ave! Using a hard ball with little or no protective kit, it was an early lesson in self-preservation.

Dad and I used to go along to watch Paul play and I had my first organised match as a fill-in. I have no great recollection of the game apart from being well down the list and being out in the field for what seemed a long, long time – early preparation for a later stint of two and a half days!

Beneath One Tree Hill, in the centre of Auckland's south-eastern suburbs, lies the Cornwall Cricket Club, one of the New Zealand game's most productive nurseries. The ground is a real rarity in that it is used solely for cricket and does not have to suffer the winter ravages of most other grounds. Players like Redmond, Martin and Jeff Crowe, Vivian and Parore have all learnt their cricket at Cornwall, under the watchful eye of people like Harold Whitcombe.

I used to write to Graham Vivian asking him when the cricket season started and he would always write back giving me the date and wishing me well. I probably knew when cricket started but just wanted to keep in contact and couldn't think of much else to ask him!

I first fronted up there at the age of nine – long socks, long shorts and long hair. I didn't play for Hogan's Heroes (the legendary team that Martin was in charge of) but soon settled in to playing early morning cricket and buying a pie and a fizzy drink off Arch MacLean after the game. Arch was one of those club men that only good clubs have – the sort of man who could never do enough for his club and who always had a kind word for any youngsters hanging around waiting for the start of the first grade game.

The only part of morning cricket I didn't enjoy was having to retire at 25, which to me didn't seem nearly enough.

I occasionally voiced my disapproval – never short of a word even then!

A couple of guys in the senior side, Rod Heath and Dave MacLean (Arch's son) took me under their wing and I felt special to think I had some mates in such high places. One day I was invited up to watch from the players' balcony and was just getting settled in when Rodney Redmond was given out to what appeared to be a "roughie". Rod and Dave suggested I move and move quickly but I left my run too late and met an enraged Redmond on the narrow staircase. It was time for a Jesse Owens impression and I just managed to get back up the stairs in time to avoid the Redmond willow which had been hurled from the top step straight into the dressing room mirror. (The mirror went everywhere – no wonder he didn't get picked again.)

It was exciting to play at a club where success prevailed and the team I watched won Auckland championships and a national one-day knock-out tournament. I wanted to play at that level and out in the middle of that great oval.

Cornwall was also the first place I ran into one M.D. Crowe, whose deeds as a youngster are well documented. His effect on me was immediate. We were playing as openers in a trial for an inter district tournament and typically he smashed it everywhere while I couldn't get it off the block – after 20-odd overs I was on about 20. After Martin was dismissed he felt I needed some cajoling and rearranged the letters on the scoreboard from GREATBATCH to HURRY UP. Not the warm, fuzzy Hogan of later years but no doubting his clarity. That team had a number of talented players and included probably New Zealand's best-ever table tennis exponent in Barry Griffiths.

Educationally I was causing ripples – not because of any rebellious streak but more a deep-seated fear of my teacher in Form I at Sacred Heart College, Miss McCready. There was a definite disconnection between us . . . and before you go thinking I was a bit soft as a youngster bear in mind she used to spook Sean Fitzpatrick and there aren't too many who can lay claim to that! I left there and went to Epsom Normal Intermediate where the new educational style suited me down to the ground. There seemed to be plenty of sport and electives and not a great deal of structure so I was in for a rude shock when I fronted up at Auckland Grammar. The sport at Epsom Normal was more of the playground type and we only occasionally pitted our skills against other schools.

As it is for many young people, secondary school was a turning point in my life. In some trepidation after hearing all the horror stories about third formers being flushed down the toilet, I fronted up and although it would be fair to say I took some time to adjust I enjoyed Auckland Grammar and all that it offered. To be honest, getting two-handed pill at the front of the lineout or punching one through the covers always held more fascination for me than, say, the role of Garibaldi in the unification of Italy.

That said, I encountered some excellent teachers and Jim Bracewell brought my mathematics to such a level that I picked up the class prize in the Fourth Form. Steve Cole was a great mate and confidante who loved talking cricket and Dave Syms instilled a certain hardness to his sporting teams, of which I was fortunate to be a member. That Dave and Steve are both headmasters is testimony to their all-round quality as professionals and as people.

There were a few odd-balls among the staff; notably Bob Hunt, who would give the boys a "birching" if we didn't get eight out of ten in his daily vocab tests. I was playing out of my skin to get seven so had to bend frequently!

The man who had the most impact on me during my time at Auckland Grammar was John Graham. I always admired the way he would treat me as a young man rather than a boy and he was always totally straight in his advice or his admonishment. Getting the call to visit 'DJ' was not usually greeted fondly but I always felt I was a better person for our discussions. Standards, discipline and excellence were what he was about and this was a big help to me as a young man who, like many of my classmates, could have taken a different path.

I was just starting my final year when I learned a very important lesson in the unlikely arena of the terraces at Eden Park. I was enjoying a beer during the one-dayer against India in 1981 when one of my mates was hit by a can. Without giving the matter much thought he picked it up and hurled it back, unfortunately under the watchful eyes of the police. It was only a matter of minutes before he was being dragged away and I thought I'd go along and ask the police where he was going so I could ring his parents.

Not surprisingly, the boys in blue didn't need my quasi-legal representation and told me to get back and watch the game. My response was ill-advised and before I knew it I was in the wagon with my mate . . . along with a group of drunks still chanting "HAD-LEE" and hammering the sides of the wagon. I had to go through the full rigmarole of finger prints and even got plonked in a cell for a few hours, the only highlight being a massive roast.

I had to front at court on the Monday, thankfully armed with a reference from John Graham which I'm sure had no little influence on my discharge. With school prefects being selected a fortnight later I felt that my chances may have been a tad slim. Thankfully those selecting the prefects (John Graham among them) felt I had something to offer and I was duly named. I had learnt an important lesson and the experience helped me become a little more measured in my actions and to realise my responsibilities as a senior sportsman at school.

My cricket had gone well at school and after a year in the top third form team (coached by both Chris Doig, now New Zealand Cricket's CEO, and Auckland rugby's Graham Henry) I made my way into the Second XI as a fourth former, keeping wicket and batting at seven or eight. We competed against the first teams from other colleges so it was a big step up playing against far more mature opposition. As my career developed this became something of a habit so it was good to be exposed to it as a youngster. Mentally I had to develop a hardness that enabled me to compete otherwise I would be buried.

This was even more obvious when I made the First XI, at that stage playing in the Senior B grade in Auckland club cricket. This was the third level down and contained a number of players either finishing their careers or moving through the club ranks. Either way, they did not like losing to the Grammar boys. Suburbs and Grafton in particular were incredibly competitive and we took special pleasure in beating them. In an astonishing three-week burst Martin Crowe scored 170, took seven for 60 and then capped it off with 240-odd. The rest of us chipped in around these performances and we won the championship and promotion to the next level.

Naturally, people thought we would fade without Hogan but we remained in the Senior A grade for many seasons. A highlight for me was making 161 against our old nemesis Grafton, made all the more pleasurable because it was after a little celebration to farewell exams for the year. The party turned out to be a late one so I was doubly determined to play well – the Grafton boys did not take kindly to an under-the-weather Greatbatch giving them a long afternoon in the field!

Another interesting opposition were University, who had in their ranks Peter McDermott and Ross Dykes; two men with whom I would have much to do in subsequent years.

My other great sporting love was rugby. I didn't play in my early years at Grammar but got serious in the sixth form and made the Second XV. The following year I made the first team and had a memorable final season of rugby. The Auckland competition is intense and we had the added pressure of playing for a team that was last defeated in 1978. The dismay of defeat in our second match was immense but in hindsight gave us the steel to remain unbeaten for the rest of the season and win the championship. Only the

World Cup team of '92 would come close to the comradeship that developed over that rugby season – we were single-minded about retaining the championship but had numerous parties after the games which brought our families into the team environment. Allan Faull was superb at keeping us tight and would often talk about family in our team meetings.

The '81 alumni from the competition feature some big names in rugby – Frano Botica, Ron Williams, Mark Brooke-Cowden, Mark Birtwistle, Sean Fitzpatrick, Bernie McCahill and Graham Dowd all lined up against us that year, as did former Auckland Warrior Se'e Solomona.

I seemed to attract trouble on the footy field as well. The King's match, an annual fixture which attracts up to 5000 people, is always an intense affair and after one scuffle their hooker didn't get up. Before I knew it, voices in the crowd were saying, "Grammar No 4, Grammar No 4, it was him!" – which didn't augur well for my chances of staying on the track. I can honestly say I had nothing to do with that particular incident but certainly tried not to take too many backward steps on a rugby field.

I locked the scrum and ended up making a few rep teams, culminating in selection for New Zealand Secondary Schools. It would have been nice to pull on the black jersey and play alongside the likes of Mike Brewer and Sean Fitzpatrick but the Springbok tour put paid to that, with the sponsor pulling out for commercial reasons.

My time at Auckland Grammar was obviously more rich in sporting endeavour than academic achievement and when I look at my chosen career I probably got the balance close to right. More importantly I was able to learn from the role models in the school and came away with a deep appreciation of the need for discipline if I was to be successful in sport and in life.

I left Auckland Grammar thankful and have always appreciated the contribution it has made in my life. Many of my classmates who hated the school while they were there now look back with due appreciation on the lessons learnt and the background it provided.

It was pretty clear that I would not be off to university so when Hogan phoned and suggested I go with him to England to play cricket I was very keen. After a few chats with people I respected I started making arrangements and organised to play for Leyland in the Lancashire league. They would find me somewhere to stay and a job and I would be their "overseas amateur".

Leyland were slow in confirming employment but I trusted them to come through and headed off to England. I hooked up with Hogan pre-season and practised with him at Bradford. After one such session we were having a pint in the clubrooms at Bradford CC when we were called in to a committee meeting and informed that the groundsman had retired and were we interested in taking the job. Leyland had yet to confirm my employment situation and I felt the chance to play with Martin on the superior facilities of the Yorkshire league was too good to turn down.

It was with some reluctance that I rang Leyland, and although they were a bit annoyed they still hadn't organised any employment so I had to go for what was certain.

Hogan had just come out of his horror first series against Australia and really struggled at the start of that season, but then regained his confidence and smashed it everywhere. I batted at six and didn't get a great deal of time out in the middle but learnt plenty from the experience and played a heap of mid-week cricket as well. I tried to play these games as hard as if they were league matches and get as much out of them as possible. Although the standard of the mid-week teams was not always that high it was important to extract maximum benefit from any game I played.

The Yorkshire lifestyle was one which I settled into with ease and talking cricket over a pint with experienced and knowledgeable players was a priceless education for an 18-year-old just out of school.

Twelve months of cricket had really helped my game

and I ended up making my first class debut at the beginning of 1983. My first experience of cricket in England merely whetted my appetite and I was back at any cost the following year. Fortunately, New Zealand were touring so I was able to assume Hogan's club professional role at Bradford.

Getting paid to play was a real thrill and I got to play on some superb grounds and against some very able cricketers. I managed to score just under a thousand runs which, although less than the Crowe runfest of the previous year, was a more than satisfactory return.

Midway through that second season with Bradford I was approached by Pudsey St Lawrence CC to be their professional. Pudsey is a famous old club in the Bradford league and boasts the great Sir Len Hutton as its most famous son. While delighted, it was a hard call to make as Bradford CC had been good to me and I had enjoyed playing with the Chadwicks and a number of other characters in the team. As a professional, though, I had to take the best offer – no-one else was going to pay me and I was soon signing up for the following year.

It would be fair to say that my time at Pudsey was the most rewarding of all my English experiences. I probably played more challenging opposition in my time with Somerset seconds, but in terms of cricket and lifestyle Pudsey was an unbeatable mix. Guys like P.C. Graham, James Dracup, Charlie Parker, Nigel Downing, Jerry Mytton and Billy Holdsworth became great mates and a good time is guaranteed whenever we get together on either side of the equator.

PC was good enough to put me up for a couple of summers, once with Lindsay Crocker and the following year with Martin Bradley. Crocks was selected to go to Zimbabwe with Jeff Crowe's Young New Zealand side but broke his arm with two games left in the season – yet another example of the cruel intervention of sporting fate as New Zealand honours were never to be offered again. Brads played a few matches for Auckland and fashioned a fine record with his off spinners . . . and to the surprise of many finished with a first class average in the thirties, largely due to an heroic knock against Michael Holding at Eden Park one day. Yorkshire and Brads were made for each other and his love of Tetley Bitter ensured bumper years for shareholders in that brewery.

We were lucky to play a few of Richard Hadlee's benefit-season matches. Lining up alongside the likes of Rice, Mudassar and Franklyn Stephenson of the West Indies was a big thrill for a couple of guys still making their way in the game.

I managed to perform well in the Bradford league, scoring a thousand runs in consecutive years and just falling short in the third year. One of the interesting quirks about cricket in Yorkshire is that if you make fifty they ring the ground collecting money for you! Although it never amounts to a fortune it's a nice little bonus for doing what they are paying you for in the first place.

Pudsey now boasts a long list of New Zealanders as old boys including Martin Crowe, Chris Pringle and Simon Doull. It was great to go back there on the 1994 tour and catch up – the club soon filled when they heard the Kiwis were back and it was special that they would come out for a pint and a chat so many years after we had played there.

If anything, league cricket taught me about hardness and adaptability. The wickets in the Bradford league, without covers and often wet, were in stark contrast to those in the Yorkshire league. Trying to play crafty old seamers and legends like Ray Illingworth was a real challenge, particularly as they knew you were the pro and a Kiwi to boot. There was real responsibility on your shoulders and the opposition didn't mind a bit of advice if they thought you were struggling.

The Yorkshiremen approach their cricket with almost religious fervour. They live and breathe the game and for a young guy with lofty ambitions it was a great finishing school. Not only was I pitted against tough opposition, but I could play and play and play, sometimes up to sixty or seventy innings a summer – stark contrast to what a developing player could expect in New Zealand.

One of the benefits of playing well as a youngster in New Zealand is that there are a number of age-group representative sides to play in. Looking back at some of these tournaments it is fascinating to see the players who have gone on to greater things not only in cricket but in other pursuits. As "Aucks" we were never the most popular competitors but I met a lot of good guys from other provinces when all the bullshit was put to one side.

Having played in a few schoolboy sides, my first "senior" rep side was the Brabin team which played in Dunedin in 1980. A couple of the guys, Richard Brazendale and Graham Jackson, were masters in the art of sledging and after we'd cleaned up Otago in two days a few of their number turned up to teach us a lesson in manners. They didn't count on our big red-headed quickie Mark Rattray, and soon were headed back to the Gardies with a different view of our cricketing etiquette! I've always been a believer in the "never take on a red-head" theory and the Otago boys soon learned why. It's funny how sledging seemed to be rife in those days – unfortunately, it seemed to affect a few guys the wrong way.

The following year I was picked for the national under-19 side which toured Australia. It was my first real taste of the Aussies and we played against the likes of McDermott, Steve Waugh, Reid and Healy. They were hard competitors as youngsters and the West Australian close fielders even spat at Tim Ritchie and me when we were batting! I think that's about as close as I'm ever likely to get to going toe to toe on a cricket field. Unbelievable stuff!

I didn't have a great tour but managed to score a ton against New South Wales in a match we ended up winning. The Aussies were on another level in most facets of their play but we managed to hang in and win a few games, and ended up around mid-table.

A player's days of age-group stuff are numbered, though, and I was soon thinking about breaking into the Auckland side. I knew I needed to have a big summer in club cricket in the 1982/83 season if I was to have the remotest chance. The Auckland team had a number of established stars from Austin Parsons to John Reid to Peter Webb and I knew that, barring injury, it would only be weight of runs that would get me a trot.

First Class Ticket

As Marc Cohn sings it, "I've got a first class ticket, but I'm as blue as a boy could be" . . . he could easily have been singing about my first few years in first class cricket. I experienced a tough introduction with the old hands of Auckland but I can look back and appreciate a little better where they were coming from. I can also compare my experiences and memories with how I would like young guys coming into the side to remember me and this has tempered the way I handle new players.

After that first season in Yorkshire I came back to New Zealand keen to build on the learning I had done. The national under-22 tournament was being held in Auckland and although I didn't set the country alight I did manage to get 130 in one game and selection in the national under-22 side. More importantly it attracted the attention of the Auckland selectors and I was picked in the squad from which the A and B sides would be selected. I was going pretty well in the club stuff and was duly selected to play for the Bs in the northern region competition against Central Districts and Northern Districts.

The CD game was a bit of a disaster and after missing out in the first innings against ND I was looking at a pretty shabby rep season. There was no more B cricket that year and my chances of breaking into the A team would be remote unless I could put together a big score. The ND bowling line-up boasted old campaigners Murray Child and Steve Scott and an up and coming quickie called Craig Presland so a big score was by no means a lay-down.

The main thing in my favour was the match venue, my home track at Cornwall Park on a lightning fast outfield. I got away to a bit of a flyer and although we lost a few wickets along the way I managed to put together a double century. It was not good enough to win the match, as former All Black Kit Fawcett hit a ton for Northern, but I thought it might be enough to get me a call. The Shell side then played two more games and I felt the season might have passed me by until chairman of selectors Eric Smith phoned and asked me to join the team for the match against Wellington. Eric had this gravelly voice that would have done Don Corleone proud and he was definitely making me an offer I couldn't refuse.

It felt strange to be taking the place of Austin Parsons, who I had gone to see bat many years ago as an admiring schoolboy. It was my turn now, and I turned up to Eden Park very early, full of nerves and raw as hell. I grabbed a little kid who had also turned up early and got him to give me throw downs for about an hour.

When it was time to go into the dressing room for the first time I hovered about waiting to see where everyone sat, petrified that I would grab someone's favourite spot and have my gear biffed into the corner. Here I was in the same dressing room as Stott, McIntyre and Cushen, having replaced their old mate Austy – nice! We had to field first which was pretty uneventful but then it was out to bat as an opener with Trevor Franklin.

Franko is a pretty relaxed character and didn't really say a lot, but he encouraged me and we almost made it through to stumps on the first day before I missed one from Evan Gray. Wellington had a useful attack and I remember the English pro Pigott bowling some pretty quick nuts. Twenty-eight was not huge but I was relieved to have at least opened my account at this level. I followed this up with another 28 in the second innings and was duly selected for the next match. No heroic "hundred on debut" stuff but solid enough and I did manage to spend quite a bit of time at the crease in each innings.

I had made it to 28 in the second dig against Northern when Barry Cooper called out "this fella hasn't made it past 28 in first class cricket yet" which put a bit of pressure on but I soon got past and ended up with 80 in my second game and felt that things were on the up and up. On the up that is until I received my first taste of cricketing factions and cliques, something which has seemed to be part of cricket in various forms in many teams I've been involved with.

We had headed down to Dunedin to take on Otago at Carisbrook, and as is typical of these sorts of clashes there was plenty of banter out on the field, with Brendon Bracewell leading the way for the Otago boys. At the end of the day Franko commented, without thinking about the fraternal objections of John, who was playing for us, that Brendon had made a bit of an arse of himself. John went ballistic but Franko stood his ground and reminded John of which team he was playing for and that he didn't give a stuff whose brother he was.

Some of the side backed Franko and others backed Braces, which meant separate dinners for the two factions that night. Things seemed back to normal the next morning but as we wandered out for warm-ups we saw at the end of the 'Brook a steamy apparition which turned out to be Braces warming up on his own. Tight lot those Bracewells!

One game remained in the season – the Shell Cup final, my first taste of one-day cricket at this level. I hared off for an outrageous single and had my poles thrown down – I was so far out your granny could have wandered in and clipped the bails off. I gained an early lesson in the differing standards between club and first class fielding and also a lesson in exercising patience and judgement.

We won the cup and at the team do after the game one of the senior players decided I would look better with a plate of savouries over my head; an action which again left me feeling unsure of myself and my standing in the team. Whether it was just a drunken act or some ill-feeling existed I didn't know, but I was quite glad to get to the end of the season and away from the environment that prevailed.

I occasionally felt like a boy among men but overall felt I belonged and just wanted to get to England, get some runs and get back for more.

I fronted up the next year for my first game, a Boxing Day limited overs affair on a green one, facing the Hadlee boys fresh from Christmas lunch at Walter's. When I strolled out to the middle the score was two for three, with Franklin, Webb and Reid back in the pavilion and Paddles pretty much on fire. His second delivery knocked my helmet off and dislodged the bails only to be called no-ball; near enough to an umpiring death-wish in Canterbury. As I started to put my lid back on a guy yelled out, "Don't worry about putting it back on, Greatbatch – he's only going to knock it off again." Considering the ease with which it had been done the first time, I had little reason to doubt him.

In the Trophy game which followed I managed to bat for nearly two hours against Hadlee, which was a real education. I could barely get it off the block but I felt if I could survive against the man whose name the press always precede with "great fast bowler" I could handle most things.

Unfortunately, second season blues set in and score-cards reading stumped Lees bowled Boock and stumped Smith bowled O'Sullivan for single figure scores became prevalent. The old campaigners would work me out and put me out of my misery. Auckland's senior players and I were still working each other out, as I was to discover after a real stuffing at the hands of Central Districts; or more particularly Martin Crowe, who scored a hundred and fifty and picked up a Michelle*.

Sean Tracy and I felt that there was little point indulging in excessive moping so grabbed a beer and headed to the showers. Unfortunately, one of the bottles hit the deck and exploded loudly, apparently simulating celebratory noises to one of the senior guys, who gave Trace and I an absolute earful about being schoolboys etcetera, etcetera. My response was equally aggressive and a naked stoush seemed on the cards, until sanity prevailed and the gentleman in question decided that rolling round on the shower floor with a nude Greatbatch would do little for his reputation as the hardman of New Zealand cricket.

Only a bash which set us on the path to victory in the rain-shortened Shell Cup final lifted the season from anything other than one of the "put that one down to experience" type.

Before the final a couple of guys I'd played cricket against in the age-group stuff, Naera Parata and Tim Ritchie, had invited me out for a beer. The first scheduled day had been rained off and as it continued to rain that night they figured a big one was in order. After the season I'd had I could ill afford to be playing climatic roulette and headed in early – very fortuitously as it turned out!

Although not a successful match for me, I did enjoy lining up against England that summer. They fielded a strong side against us and playing on the same park as Botham, Gower and Lamb was very exciting for a young guy. Having to face Willis, Dilley and Foster was less exciting but I managed to bat for an hour against them in the second dig which was something of a personal triumph, even if they were only going at three-quarter pace.

Two seasons in, I'd had nearly twenty bats for an average of twenty so it would be fair to say the New Zealand incumbents were not lying awake at night thinking about

---

*Pfeiffer – a fivefer

M.J. Greatbatch. I found Sneds and Braces bloody hard work. It seemed like I just couldn't take a trick with those two and although it may have helped my game from a mental hardness point of view, I think I would have prospered more with some encouragement at times. That's not a knock on those guys because we get on fine these days but I'd be lying if I said I didn't find them a bit daunting.

Ironically it was against Central Districts in 1985/86 that I finally made a real impression in first class cricket, although if it wasn't for the good sportsmanship of Scott Briasco I would have had to wait even longer. When I nicked one to him at second slip early in my innings everyone went up, the umpires confirmed the appeal and I began the trudge off. Scotty then called me back – a great gesture and one that I have since learnt typifies the guy. It was also a gesture which earnt him plenty of stick from his teammates as I went on to score my maiden first class hundred.

We were set a stiff chase in the second innings and I had the misfortune to run-out the skipper, Peter Webb. As Webby walked past he growled, "Don't come back until you've won this game" – good incentive to stay out there and knock them off! A double of a hundred and an eighty not out to win the game were two important milestones. Obviously the first hundred is important, but to bat through and knock off a total was also a notable hurdle to clear.

The season stats point to a pretty good year with 300 runs at 39; but take away the 200 I scored in one game and my battles with inconsistency are seen to remain. I still didn't feel like an established player and my record shows that I got to fifty just five times in forty innings, which is poop for a batsman in the top five. I knew that the test players would be around more the following season and there was little to suggest permanence about my Auckland spot.

A phone call from Brian Jewell, chairman of the Central Districts selectors, and a chat with Hogan, who was now based in Hastings, convinced me that perhaps my future in first class cricket lay elsewhere.

Most sporting administrations of the time were run by enthusiasts rather than by professionals so it would be unfair to cite administration as a reason for dissatisfaction with Auckland Cricket. Auckland had supported me financially as a young player and I was grateful to them for that. The fact of the matter was that I wasn't enjoying my cricket and my results and demeanour reflected this. I had batted in every spot in the top five; not the perfect career path for a young guy. Sure, you take your chance when first selected and bat where you can but three and a half seasons of floating up and down the order meant I wasn't sure of my best spot and it was pretty obvious the selectors didn't know either.

I was invited down to Hawke's Bay to get a feel for the place and was put up with Basil and Jan Dynan, who certainly sold me on the area. John Wiltshire phoned while I was down and we began to organise employment and accommodation. Employed at Hastings Boys' High as a "tutor", I have a sneaking suspicion that some of the lads may not have as comprehensive an understanding of the origins of World War Two than if someone else had been in charge. Having said that, their ability to leg glance may have suffered under a different tutor so it cuts both ways!

I played my club cricket for Hastings Old Boys and got opportunities for U-Bix Cup matches as well. There was a far greater emphasis on cricket, the wickets were good but there was a relaxed approach and great support from the local people. One of the sponsors found a flat for me above a pub (Braggs Bar & Grill) and I was set.

I made some runs early on and was named in the Central Districts squad. At the first meeting for the year Brian Jewell informed me that I would bat three for the season, which just blew me away after the "think of a number, subtract two and put your pads on" approach I had experienced with Auckland. Although I understood my permanence was contingent on form, I was hugely motivated by such a strong belief in me. Brian was as good as his word as I had a pretty ordinary Cup run but he stuck with me and I came right in the Trophy. With a different selection philosophy I may have been lucky to be retained.

There was a real difference in the feeling of team unity and we all pulled hard for each other throughout the season. Our tactics were very clear and everyone knew the role that was expected of them. We would endeavour to bat first on all but the greenest tracks and try and score about 350 with an hour to go on day one. It meant we had two cracks with a fresh new ball attack and advanced the game sufficiently to mean an outright result was possible for both sides.

I broke the Central Districts record for most runs in a season, which I was pretty chuffed about, but unfortunately Hogan decided to double it! I had scored three hundreds and felt like I was now a fully fledged first class cricketer but most importantly I was enjoying the camaraderie and the unity among the team.

We ended up winning the Trophy for the first time in Central Districts' history after a memorable victory over Canterbury at Pukekura Park. Having been set 375 at five an over (Shake always hated losing), Hogan and I both got tons to secure victory. It was a brilliant moment and although Hogan was dominant all the guys knew they had contributed. Along with the '92 World Cup side it was the best cricket team unit I have been involved with.

My only brush with international cricket that summer was a match on my new home ground, McLean Park, Napier, against the touring West Indians. Selection for a Shell XI was the first indication that the national selectors had some time for me. My first opportunity to lay claim to higher honours was presented to me but Joel Garner brushed me aside through the safe hands of Richie Richardson at slip. As a young guy I used to read about players naming Joel as their most difficult opponent and as his 6ft 8in frame came sauntering in I could see why.

It was also my first opportunity to see the great Viv Richards in the flesh and although Danny hurried him a couple of times he smashed a superb century. I was fielding at mid-on and he kept nudging it to my right and ambling down the wicket, daring me to have a flick at the stumps. Once he hit it a bit hard and I had it in my hand with Viv about four yards down. I motioned to throw and he just stared at me and said "Go on Man", making no attempt to get back in his ground. I just stood there, mesmerised by his arrogance.

Over thirteen seasons of first class cricket I have been lucky enough to play with and against a number of guys with differing styles, habits and personality traits.

I played a heap of my early cricket with Sean Tracy, who ended up representing Auckland, Canterbury and Otago before he finished. Trace was raw and just loved bowling fast and it was a shame that he didn't make more of an impression on the international stage. I think at times he was in too much of a hurry but it was pointless trying to change him.

Two guys who played a bit of cricket with and against me up in Yorkshire were Martin Pringle and Martin Bradley. We were fiercely competitive but enjoyed some great times up there, although driving around in my old Fiat reduced both of them to white-knuckled terror from time to time. Both of them put together some good performances for Auckland but I'm sure would have benefited from more regular play, which they would have surely got in most other provinces. Ian Fisher was another who started with Auckland and made the move to CD. Fish was a real competitor and hit the seam more than most, but always had a grin on his face as six o'clock approached – he certainly knew how to enjoy a night out.

Peter Webb was a senior member of the Auckland side when I was first picked and became something of a father figure to me. We were both playing for Cornwall and he would spend many hours talking cricket and helping me with my game. Mentally he helped me a lot, particularly about pacing innings and what to expect at the next level.

After a nightmare introduction to test cricket, he was unlucky not to be given another shot. His last international experience was a one-dayer against England, before which he turned up at a champagne breakfast I was having, had half a glass of champers and went off to take on the Poms!

Trevor Franklin was another guy who I used to really enjoy being around. If ever there were a couple of different options in terms of dinner or activities on tour, Franko and I would always find ourselves in the same group. I believe he was omitted too early from the national side – his opening combination with John Wright is still the most prolific in New Zealand history in terms of century stands. To achieve as he did after the crippling injury he suffered at Heathrow speaks more eloquently about the courage of the man than I ever could.

Dipak Patel played his first season for Auckland in my last year but was really good to me, spending hours teaching me how to sweep. I really appreciated this sort of attention and as an experienced county pro he was great to practise with and learn from. I didn't expect him to give me advice on my shaving technique, but one day I was having a shave after a game and he was horrified at my method. Dipak being a smooth dude, I adjusted accordingly.

The Otago side of the mid to late eighties had an equal mixture of talent and competitive edge. Wally Lees was a good talker behind the sticks and was always forthcoming with advice about my batting . . . it seemed like nothing had changed when he took over the coaching role, although his later advice was a little more constructive!

The Lees-Boock partnership is legendary and Boocky had such great control it was difficult to get a run off him at times. When you're a young guy desperate to succeed and surrounded by Lees, McCullum and the Blair brothers with Boocky landing it on a handkerchief, survival, let alone run-getting, is a huge challenge.

Another Otagoite who I had a bit of fun with was J.A.J. Cushen. Cush didn't really take to me much when we were in the same side (he probably thought I was just a snotty-nosed schoolboy), but strangely we got along okay when in opposition. This camaraderie didn't extend to the field, however, and I was just another batsman that he wanted to get rid of. After the game he was always good for a beer and once took me out sailing, which is his other great love. When I was first in the Auckland side, Cush lived on Waiheke and used to sail to training – I don't think he made it home too many times!

Discussion about characters in New Zealand cricket would be incomplete without a Chris Kuggeleijn story. On tours of India there is always potential for a bit of boredom and Kuggs came up with a scheme to relieve us not only of our boredom but also of a substantial amount of our tour income as well. Having married into a horse-breeding family, Kuggs felt it would be entertaining for us to look at tapes of some of the family horses that were for sale. Before long he'd convinced us that if we purchased this horse a trip to Flemington in November was almost a dead cert and we should book early to avoid disappointment.

Without a moment's hesitation we were showering Kuggs with money and Flying Willow was ours, a champion in the making and a small fortune just around the corner. Unfortunately, a game sixth at Waipa was the best result returned. The only thing that helped my humour was that canny investor R.J. Hadlee bought two shares! It still probably hurt me more than him.

I didn't get too close to many of the Wellington guys but I have vivid recollections of Erv McSweeney. Perhaps it's just a gloveman's thing, but I thought he was one of the most niggly guys I ever played against. He was always competing hard and letting you know if he thought you weren't in great nick. Like most characters of that ilk it made you doubly determined to knock him over but I think we came out about even over the years.

Current Wellingtonian but former Cantabrian Richard Petrie was an interesting proposition, at times appearing to have two personalities. It wasn't only with ball in hand that he went a little odd but I do recall him playing his first one-dayer against Australia at the SCG. After an understandably nervous beginning he beat the bat a couple of times and started to give a bit of lip to Allan Border, only about 200 games more experienced. Border looked over at Martin Crowe in the covers and asked, "Where did you get this one from?"

Petrie's new-ball partner in Canterbury was Stu Roberts. If they picked touring teams on ability to inject humour into proceedings, Stu would be first man picked every time. On the tour of Pakistan his "prayer sessions" were legendary and he was a vital man to have about on such a tough tour. Even though he wasn't playing, he kept the team spirits up; mind you, the fact that he wasn't playing and didn't have to face a lethal Waqar might have had something to do with his good humour!

Tony Blain would be one of the nicest guys I've played with and was a guy you could rely on regardless of the situation. If ever the guys needed a lift Blainy would provide it and he was a bloody good cricketer. He bore the brunt of being the only 'keeper on the tour to Australia in 1993/94 and was exhausted by the end of the domestic series against Pakistan. Typically, he just gutsed it out but his form suffered in the end. His appointment to the coach's role in Auckland will bring a different dimension to that side and should provide a good complement to the disciplines and structure that Braces has put in place.

Much of my early time in the Bay was spent with John Wiltshire as he got me organised and sorted out all the little settling-in details. John has always been a great supporter and had a knack of finding the right words, whether of encouragement or admonition. Experience as captain of two provincial sides meant he had a vast store of experience to hand on and we had many evenings discussing cricket over a red wine or two.

Hawke's Bay sport would be the poorer were it not for

the efforts of Blair Furlong over many years. When I first arrived I was told his name was Brian and spent the first half of the summer having my cheerful "G'day Brian" greeting returned with a half scowl and cursory nod of the head . . . I thought he was a bit odd until someone put me straight. Blair has put a heap into cricket and I'm sure takes great pleasure seeing his sons John and Campbell enjoy the facilities he has worked so hard to provide.

I always felt the Central boys played their best cricket "on the road", as the basketballers say. When we got together and played two or three games on the trot, we developed a close family kind of feeling and success in that environment is always more rewarding. Scotty Briasco was always the steady eddie of the side who tempered the more ebullient personalities of the Blains and the Stirlings. With well over 4000 runs in first class cricket, Scotty's record is among the finest of any CD batsman.

The two quicks, Garry Robertson and Derek Stirling, were not only very fine bowlers but a lethal pair off the track as well. They seemed to stick together and were a constant source of good humour, with Stirls' mimicry frequently having the boys rolling around. Stu Duff was another great servant of CD cricket and a search of the record books will reveal that very few other players have scored 3000 runs and taken 200 wickets for their province. Duffy has taken to the golf course with the same dedication and intensity he displayed in his cricket, so don't be surprised to see him make a name for himself there.

My best mate in CD cricket would have been Roger Twose. Twosey is a brilliant individual who gives and gives and gives to any side he plays for. Ultra-competitive, he will turn anything into a game and as I'm not keen on losing either we have had some titanic battles over the most bizarre things. His decision to turn down a huge contract from Warwickshire was based as much on his love for New Zealand than on any desire to play test cricket.

Twosey is passionate about New Zealand, his girlfriend

is a New Zealander and he really enjoys the country and its people.

Of the younger guys, Simon "Ces" Wilson is a guy with immense talent and a super technique but just hasn't quite leapt the hurdle to become a consistent first class player. Ces is a real character and on one trip was doing the typical scarfie thing and leading the drinking on the bus home. We stopped for takeaways along the way and it didn't take long before the inebriation took hold and Ces had covered his fish and chips in a sauce of his own making. The events that followed are better left unreported; suffice to say he must have been very hungry!

Glen Sulzberger had a great first year which I think comes back to having to work hard and play a lot of good cricket before he made his first class debut. The work he had put in gave him a hardness that meant he was mentally ready for the step up. If he continues to progress but is not rushed he could go all the way. The other young guys like Matthew Walker, Jacob Oram, Campbell Furlong and Andrew Penn are all very talented and I would love to work with them and help them with their development.

It is important that players do serve some form of apprenticeship and have a formal mentoring system which will give them help in preparing for the various levels they must succeed at if they are to not only reach test level but be successful test players.

The Real Thing

At the end of January 1987 I learned that I had been awarded the Lowe Walker scholarship to play for the Somerset Second team for a season. It was the first year of an exchange programme which has been of immense value to Central Districts and, I would like to think, has made a reasonable contribution to Somerset cricket as well.

Graeme Lowe put his company's support behind the project and it was to be the first of many associations with Graeme and his extraordinary support for sport in the Bay and other parts of New Zealand. It was a very exciting proposition and although I was going to miss my mates up in Yorkshire the thought of being completely immersed in a professional cricketing environment was irresistible.

Martin Crowe was the county professional and bearing the strain over the sacking of the West Indian greats Richards and Garner. Peter Roebuck was the captain of the side and he and Martin were definitely seen as the villains in the early part of that season. I threw myself into the experience and loved the thought of playing or practising every day of the week. Even if there was no match on I was expected to turn up and practise and there were always plenty of net bowlers on hand. The only downside was not being able to play for the seconds in their one-day league, but on those occasions I was 12th for the top side – a great learning experience.

The club were looking for a place for Hogan and because we were good mates decided to get somewhere big enough for the both of us. Ironically it was in a little village called Crowcombe, about fifteen minutes from the ground. Our house was in the middle of a big farm, perfect for training runs, and not too far from the Farmers Arms where a pint of Guinness and a pub meal were an "occasional" pleasure.

The head coach of Somerset was the former England test player Brian Rose and as a knowledgeable guy and, more particularly, a left-hander was great value throughout the year. Peter Robinson (a former left arm spinner for the club) looked after the seconds and always ensured I got maximum value out of every net. I would turn up to practice early and Robbo would work his wiles on me with 15 imaginary fielders around the bat and 28 ways to get out – brilliant experience and an important extra that the other guys weren't getting.

Two old heads from Somerset that I got on really well with were Nigel Felton and Trevor Gard. They had both played many years for the club and it was great to be invited into their homes or out for a pint or two. Trev was the typical "Zummerset" lad with the full "orright Batchy boy, hars it gooin then lud" type of accent. As a good mate of Botham's he'd seen some great sights on both sides of the boundary rope.

I was put in charge of the second side which made me think a bit harder about my game and added some responsibility to my batting. In the weekends I played out at Clevedon, which supplemented my diet of three-day stuff – important because I only had 19 bats for the twos. It was extremely satisfying to average over fifty and line up against a couple of real quicks for the first time. Ricky Ellcock and Tony Merrick, both West Indians, were another speed altogether from what I had been used to and Merrick in particular really made you sniff it. I got out to him gloving one that had I missed would have meant cosmetic reconstruction. Ellcock went on to play for England before back problems got the better of him and Merrick had a few games for the Windies. At that stage of my career I thought they were the fastest things breathing.

Midway through the year and midway through a match against Kent I received a letter from the New Zealand Cricket Council saying I had been selected as one of a twenty-strong squad to prepare for the 1987 World Cup. It was my first "selection" at that level and I was over the moon – apart from the Shell game against the Windies I had had no real inkling of interest from Mr Neely and Co and now I was clearly in their plans. My delight was tempered a little by a line in the letter which read "even though you are unlikely to make the final 14". At least it wasn't just a form letter – I can't imagine Hogan's saying that!

The effect the letter had on me was remarkable in terms of the self-imposed pressure I began to experience. I kept thinking "you're in the top twenty players in New Zealand now, so you'd better perform like it". Of course, the Somerset guys had all heard the news so I wanted to prove myself to them as well. As it happens, in my next innings I went out and played like a drunk, the more I thought about it the worse I got and I finally got out for an innings far from befitting a World Cup squad member.

Before returning to take part in the World Cup training camp I underwent a very important part of my preparation for the following summer. I teamed up with my old Cornwall buddy (and later Auckland selector) Rex Smith and headed off on a Kontiki tour. "Old" was the operative word for Smithy, given that only a very liberal interpretation of what "18–35-year-olds" means allowed him to take his place on the tour. Kontiki tours usually have connotations of wild extramurality and claims of preparation for a cricket season may seem a tad spurious.

Thankfully, Rex was a keen runner and we ran and ran and ran through the streets of Europe's famous cities, culminating in the impromptu Tour de Roma back to our camping ground on the hills outside the eternal city. It was near the end of the trip and because we were feeling fit we thought a decent run of about ninety minutes would be a good way to round off our training. Regrettably, our fitness did not match our sense of direction and it was a couple of very jaded boys who shuffled into the campsite two and a half hours later!

On my return to New Zealand I was straight into a three-day camp with the World Cup squad, which would not normally warrant a mention but for the clear undercurrent of animosity between coach Glenn Turner and a number of the senior players. I enjoyed the camp and was really impressed with Turner's organisational and technical skills but the criticisms of the man during his second term as coach were being made nearly ten years earlier.

As the letter predicted, I missed the final squad and settled down to the first class season in the knowledge that only a big pile of runs or some disastrous form from the incumbents was going to get me in. I was not prepared to leave it up to someone else, though, and began compiling runs fairly consistently.

There have been numerous debates about the value of overseas players in domestic cricket and that season I had an experience which put me firmly in the supporters' camp. We were playing Canterbury on a lively track at Horton Park, Blenheim, and charging in was the West Indian legend Michael Holding. Using all the experience gained while collecting 249 test scalps, Holding bowled over the wicket, round the wicket and used his full repertoire on me. He would set an attacking field and bowl in a way which made it quite clear to me as a batsman how he was trying to get me out. It was as if he was saying, "Righto sonny, we both know what I'm trying to do – are you good enough to survive?" Actually it was probably "Righto man" but that's not important. I managed to not only survive but also to get a hundred and it was another hurdle in preparing me for test cricket.

Being picked for the Shell XI was a good sign, but obviously runs were the requirement. I had a pretty average match so it was with some surprise that I was asked to join the twelve to go to Christchurch to play England in the first test. I had made it but don't recall great emotion – things were happening pretty quickly and it was a very exciting time.

However, it was something I had worked towards and I felt I had served my apprenticeship. I had one challenge left in terms of selection and that was to make the XI. Before the test we all dressed in our "number ones" for the team dinner, a practice which, sadly, has been discontinued. It was a proud moment to receive my test cap and at that stage I felt I had a good chance of playing, the balance of the side being such that if I didn't play John Bracewell would have to bat six, which would have been unusual.

The dinner finished relatively early and we went back to the hotel at about 9.30. Sitting alone in my room at the Camelot Court I soon became desperate for company and as the nerves got the better of me I found myself hammering on Franko's door. The ensuing chat and cup of tea were just what I needed to calm down and collect my thoughts – Franko, as ever, proving to be a good mate in time of need.

It would be fair to say that I'm no stranger to a knife and fork but the nerves were still there in the morning and the sight of Stockley sailing into a cooked brekky – the full bacon, egg, sausage, tomato and hash brown number – nearly made me chuck.

Standing in the famous dressing rooms at Lancaster Park, I did the "new boy thing" and stood around waiting to see which space was left over, in exactly the same manner as I had minced around the Auckland dressing room five years earlier. I was particularly keen not to take the great fast bowler's spot, which would have been tantamount to sacrilege, probably treasonable, at his home deck.

Ten o'clock rolled round and I figured by now I was playing but within moments Chopper came up and asked me to carry the drinks, the euphemism for five days of being the team "gofer". Not that I minded, though, as I could settle in to being part of the test scene without the responsibility of putting an innings together.

As it happened, Paddles pinged a calf in the first session and I got to field for the rest of the match. It was a real shame for him and one of the few times in his career when his performance didn't match the script –he was poised to own outright the test wicket-taking record – but it meant I could really get involved. I managed to pick up a couple of catches and finished the match comfortable about being part of things, with the jitters of the Camelot Court well behind me.

Paddles was obviously out of the next test and Andrew Jones had broken a wrist during the game so I knew for certain that the next major hurdle of my career was upon me – having a bat in a test match.

As a fourth former at Auckland Grammar I was one of many lads who had gathered around the various televisions the school had organised to witness the first ever victory over England in test cricket. It was one of those strange pieces of sporting fate that almost exactly ten years later I was taking on England with another who had huddled around the TV in 1978, Martin Crowe.

Chopper won the toss and we had a bat, which meant a bit of a wait, but shortly after tea on the first day I was striding out to face my first ball in test cricket. People have commented on my eagerness to get out to the middle, often beating the outgoing batsman through the gate. I've always thought it better to display a sense of wanting to be out there and competing rather than waiting until the fieldsmen

J.G. Blackwell

Cover driving at Perth – a sweet feeling.

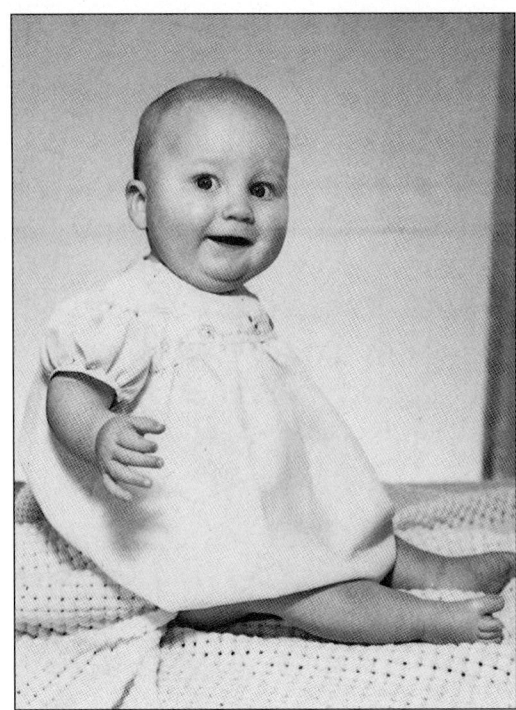

Greatbatch Collection

M. Greatbatch 1964 version.

Greatbatch Collection

The '75 Cornwall reps – with Hogan, Grubby De Groen and Dave 'The Goose' Crowe.

Clive Ralph

A great bunch of guys – always proud to don the stag.

All Sport/Simon Bruty

Drinks waiters – Greatbatch and Fairbrother – Christchurch 1988.

J.G. Blackwell

With the hero of Perth – Martin Snedden.

J.G. Blackwell

Batting against Pakistan, with encouragement from Javed at silly point.

Visual Impact/Richard Hare

Leading the victory dance – another scalp for Dipak.

All-Sport/Simon Bruty

If the cap fits . . .

All-Sport/Simon Bruty

On the field for the first time in a test – Braces you beauty!

All-Sport/Simon Bruty

Jeez, I didn't get near that – I wonder if I should show him how it feels when I really do hit something.

J.G. Blackwell

Punching one for four, v India, Eden Park 1990.

begin contemplating "timed out" appeals. Dilley was running in at me and as a new boy they popped in a short point just to add a bit of pressure. Thankfully I managed to push one just wide of cover and the test run account was officially open.

I managed to bat through to stumps and was there when Wrighty brought up his hundred – his joy at reaching three figures remains with me and it was a feeling I was desperate to share. After batting for about an hour (which was bloody hard work) I got a little touch on one from Dilley and contemplated standing but Fred Goodall gave me out with the sort of speed usually reserved for Hadlee victims at Lancaster Park.

Although out for 11 I didn't feel out of my depth and was determined to maintain a philosophy of learning from the innings but not getting myself down and stewing over what might have been. I can remember thinking "Right, I'll get some next dig" which is a good indication of my state of mind. I'd played about thirty first class games at that stage so had a reasonable amount of experience to draw on. In stark contrast, some of the newer additions to the New Zealand side when struggling with their game do not have a lot of cricket life behind them.

England got their nose in front and we knew we had to play well to keep the game safe, but Franko and Wrighty put on a hundred and it seemed any opportunity for a long bat would have to wait until the next test. Suddenly, we plummeted from 117 without loss to 119 for three and before too much longer 153 for five. As I settled in with Sneds (there as nightwatchman) there was plenty of batting to do if we were to save the match. We made it to stumps OK but faced a huge task the following day with not a great deal of batting left and me, an unproven debutant, as the only remaining specialist batsman.

There's no question it was a pretty flat old track and the majority of the England attack were more "solid county pro" than the upper echelon of test cricket material. Jarvis,

Radford and Capel were all good bowlers, but were not the sort of guys who should unduly trouble you on a lifeless Eden Park. The two who stood out were Dilley and Emburey; Dilley for his extra speed and movement and Emburey not so much for prodigious turn but for his ability to keep making you play and play, leaving very little to kick away or leave.

When I think about my introduction to test cricket, and compare it with the starts presented to Hogan and Rutherford, I guess I was pretty lucky. Having to start against Lillee, Thomson, Marshall and Garner would have been quite different, and their lack of experience at the time of their debuts meant they had nothing to refer to in terms of a cricketing memory bank. The other thing in my favour was that my responsibility was simply to bat – no run rate to think of, no targets to set – JUST BAT.

I probably took all that a bit literally and it was three hours or so before I pushed Emburey backward of square to bring up my first fifty in test cricket. It was a nice feeling but a half century was going to neither save the game nor guarantee a trip to Wellington for the next test so it was head down, bum up and on with it. By now Braces had joined me and he was fantastic, giving a lot of encouragement and keeping me working hard. Braces is a funny mixture, sometimes abrasive and sometimes empathetic, but during test matches he was definitely one to have inside the tent.

A solid diet of Emburey, accompanied by Gatting's "dibbly dobblers", meant I could don the black cap, which doesn't happen too often in test cricket. The cap is a real icon of tradition and has been superseded by more practical headwear but I always get a thrill out of wearing it and to be able to in my first test was a great feeling.

Being in Auckland, I had plenty of mates in the Park and every now and then I would hear shouts of support. I would like to apologise to the guy who yelled out "You've got a bat – use it", who clearly objected to my methods. The remark didn't get to me but after punching Emburey for four through point (one actually bounced high enough to cut) I was in the 70s and a debut hundred beckoned. My problem was that if I continued at the rate I was playing it would be about the time they identified the murderer in that night's *Taggart* that I would reach three figures. The big clock that used to sit over the old No 3 stand was taunting me and it wasn't long before I had a huge heave at Gatting, thankfully landing it between the two guys in the deep. The escape got my head back in order and a realisation that the 22 runs I needed would come – I just needed to stick there.

Braces got out to Gatting and Smithy came out and made a mockery of my funereal rate by whistling it everywhere in a typical cameo – he was looking to bring up a thousand runs in test cricket and while not a big milestones man he was keen to knock them off.

I continued to labour away and although very fit that summer I was also very tired. It had been as long as I'd batted at that stage of my career and once into the nineties I thought, "Right, if Emburey lands it on leg I'm having a go." It was an over or two's wait but finally there it was and I heaved it over mid-wicket for four. I'd done it, but before I could get too carried away Stockley was shaking my hand and congratulating me but saying, "It'll feel a lot better if you're here at the end." He was dead right so I had to settle back down when I really just wanted to sail into a beer or two.

A mate of mine, Antony Sumich, charged out on to the field and pumped my hand with a "Well done big fella" – it was tempting to follow him back to the terraces!

Coming off I was greeted with a pretty flat dressing room which I found puzzling until it was revealed that Chopper had been replaced as captain. It was a real shame as all the guys had a heap of respect for Jeff but the selectors couldn't stick with him and Wrighty took over as captain. Sure, I had a couple of beers that day but it was a personal triumph and not one that the team could get overly excited about. We'd drawn a pretty dull test and the skipper had been dropped – not the traditional recipe for dressing room frivolity.

We were travelling the next day and playing the day after so it was business as usual pretty quickly. It actually suited me, because any sportsman in form just wants to play and play and the thought of another bat on what promised to be an easy-paced Basin wicket was very tasty indeed. As it happens I blew a chance of back to back hundreds but was happy enough to have a century and a fifty to my name after two tests. John Wright had come in after his first session in test cricket thinking "If that's test cricket you can stick it" so by comparison I enjoyed a dream introduction.

I loved those first few weeks as an international player. It was what I had worked hard for and playing against England at home was a happy beginning. But was I really there? I hadn't played against the Aussies, the Windies, India or the Pakis and in my heart I knew I still had much in front of me before I could say I truly belonged at test level. It was nice, though, knowing that if I fell under a bus that winter, M.J. Greatbatch 107 n.o. v England would be there forever.

Runs in the Sun

I arrived in India having had a lot of cricket in 1988. I'd made my test debut, played a season with Yeadon up in Yorkshire, travelled to Zimbabwe with the Young New Zealand side and here I was in Bombay ready for my first tour with the New Zealand cricket team. People make a big deal out of your first test, and rightly so, but the first tour is also a big moment in any player's career.

Over many tours, New Zealand had beaten India only once so we knew we had some tough cricket to play if we were to be successful. Off the field there were a number of challenges to be faced, not the least of which is the restricted diet, which to a good tooth man is tough going on a seven-week tour. Martin Crowe was unavailable because of ill health (he seems to have recovered well from the AIDS he was reportedly afflicted with) but the great fast bowler was there, keen to break Botham's record and become the greatest wicket taker in test history.

Without wanting to do a Clive James, I found India to be a nation of contrasts – from the beautiful to the grotesque, from the wealthy to the destitute – and from the outset we knew we were in a country so different from our own it was as if cricket was the only thing we had in common. The late night bus trip from the airport to our hotel in Bombay was frequented by splashes of light revealing families living on the side of the road in tenuously constructed shelters. Within moments we were in the Taj Palace; one of the most splendid hotels I have ever been in, with restaurants, shops, health clubs – everything you could wish for in a luxury establishment.

Rajkot was the venue for the first game and as we made our way from the airport into town we noticed a large billboard announcing "THE 5 STAR JAYSON HOTEL WELCOMES THE NEW ZEALAND CRICKET TEAM". We were all pretty excited by this and thought it was great that they were making such a big deal of our arrival. As we got closer, the town was starting to do a remarkable impression of a biblical scene but things were on the improve as we pulled up outside the hotel.

We were greeted as we got off the bus with the traditional string of flowers and the dot of dye to the forehead. Not all the boys were too keen on the dye as it was a hell of a job to wash it off.

As we entered the hotel, the land of contrasts hit us again – the hotel was as far removed from the Taj Palace as you could imagine and how they got five stars remains a mystery. The lift was a hand-pulled number and as Stockley and I were rooming together we decided it would be more prudent to take the stairs. The room had two bunks, a bowl in the corner and a concrete floor – it was as if there was a shortage of accommodation in the town and they'd cleaned out the local prison to make room for us. "Welcome, Batchy," said Stockley as he reclined on his bunk, "welcome to international cricket!"

The rooms may not have been much but the service was unbelievable. It seemed like there was a man on every door who would dart around all over the place, making sure our every need was met. Although keen to get into the game, we were soon to discover our gear had been delayed. Margot Butcher was reporting on the tour and decided to travel with the team kit, which was being transported by truck to give the plane a better shot of going the distance. Unfortunately, they ran over a villager on the way up and there was a lot of sorting out to do before they were allowed to resume their journey. Our bags arrived in time for us to get a start at about three o'clock on the first day!

The night before the game we all dined on the roof. It was fun to sit there looking out over Rajkot and I remember vividly the sound of the local dentist drilling away after hours. Those team meals were a real feature of the tour and because they were informal and relaxed we all had a great time at them. It is one of the beauties of being in a country like India that the team does tend to stay together more, rather than different groups popping out to different pubs or restaurants, as happens in England or Australia.

Paddles showed he was ready to get amongst it with an astonishing display of bowling, picking up 9-55 on a very unresponsive track. I took off to get the milk but forgot to close the gate and my bails were whipped off smartly, out stumped in my first knock in India. If you're going to get stumped I guess India is the appropriate place, but I was looking for greater things with only one more match before the first test.

We took off to Kapil Dev country for the next match where Shake picked up his second hundred in a row. I picked up my second failure in a row and wasn't in great nick as we approached the test. It was a tough way to get ready for the tests – very little cricket really and only Shake and Franko had put together reasonable back-to-back digs.

For a number of reasons, the test match was a big occasion. It was my first test away from New Zealand, and it was also the test in which Richard Hadlee was attempting to break the Botham record. The other reason was simply that it was in India, a nation of cricket nuts who turn up in big numbers. They love to set off fire crackers in the stand which, for a team of already indifferent bowel control, was a major challenge. The spectators were warm and friendly for the most part, and although they hadn't heard of too many of us I think they admired the way we played the game.

We had a bowl and Stockley, me at first, Braces at second and Kuggs at third all waited nervously for the historic nick. Not surprisingly with Stockley and Kuggs there, a couple of wagers were made as to who would be the recipient. We didn't have to wait too long before Arun Lal nicked one and Kuggs snaffled it with ease – a pretty big catch to take twenty minutes into your first test. Paddles cleaned up Srikkanth and we were in good shape early on, but Sidhu and Vengsarkar put together a good partnership and they ended up a few short of four hundred.

In one over just after lunch, Sidhu, in an amazing display of clean, powerful hitting, hit Evan Gray for three sixes. The way he played the spinners was a real education; he was looking to dominate from the start rather than trying to defend and preserve in the way we were. I fielded at silly point for much of the tour which is a bit like being a coconut at the fairground.

They opened with Dev and Ayub, who bowled quick "fizzy" little offies with great accuracy. All of our batsmen batted for reasonably long periods of time but none of us really took the game to them. After a good start, we collapsed a little to be 145-6 going into the rest day.

On the eve of the rest day we had an official function and after Plums (who was the tour food Nazi) gave the spread the once over we all enjoyed the hospitality. I felt a bit dodgy that night but was not prepared for what was to greet me in the morning. As a member of the social committee I had organised a tennis tournament for the day off and popped down for a bit of brekky. I was baffled to find that no-one else was lining up. I went up to see Plums and he told me that we had a major with most of the team afflicted with severe vomiting and diarrhoea. I wasn't a hundred percent but was in rude health compared with the likes of Kuggs and Paddles. I think only Stockley managed to escape completely, testament to his iron constitution. The Bombay Open was going to have to wait as more and more crosses were taped to our hotel room doors.

My roommate was Ken Rutherford, who was severely afflicted, to the extent that he left a load on my number ones. I was sympathetic to his illness but thought it well on the nose that he didn't front for my laundry bill.

The next day a lot of the guys showed a great deal of courage just to get to the ground. Kuggs came out to bat in his first test in an awful state and missed a straight one from Kapil for a first baller. It was a cruel start for a great team man and one of the real personalities of New Zealand cricket.

Probably the only guy sicker than Kuggs was Paddles and he was next in. Finding it difficult even to stand he slashed at one from Kapil and got us past the follow on. It was a great performance from those guys and bought us a little more time. The Indians tore into our three-man bowling attack leaving us 340 to win in a day and a bit. We had fielded for only a couple of hours but it felt like a couple of days.

Thankfully Shake and Franko continued their good form and got us through to 70 without loss at stumps. The pitch was starting to do all sorts and although we had made a good start we were under no illusions about the challenge on the final day. From the moment we lost Franko we were never really in it, and finished off losing the last ten wickets for 87 runs. Only Stockley got into twenties and we knew we had a heap of work to do just to remain competitive, let alone have a chance of winning.

We were up against it but the team seemed to bond well – we made the most of the team room, which was a big area on a different floor from the rooms we were sharing. Whether it was to watch a video, have a beer or just to escape the confines of your hotel room, the team room was a great place to unwind.

I missed out again in the first dig against Tamil Nadu and at that stage had five scores under twenty for the tour. Thankfully we got another bat and I finally got to fifty, which was a huge boost leading up to the test. It was certainly a sharp learning curve for me, and I was starting to feel more positive about playing them – Sidhu and Srikkanth definitely demonstrated a method of playing spinners based on gaining the ascendancy early and not letting the bowler dictate terms. While I wasn't about to hare off down the track and try to whang it into the stands like those boys, I was determined to use my bat more, to hit every ball, rather than get obsessed with kicking it away.

We stepped out up at Bombay acutely aware of the challenge which was in front of us. The expectation of the Indian public was that they would continue to dominate us – their batsmen had been playing very aggressively and their spinners definitely had the upper hand. It was crunch time, but at last we had a full strength side to pick from.

Our first impressions of the deck were less than encouraging and it looked badly underprepared. The ball can seam a bit in Bombay but the state of the wicket encouraged Shake to have a bat – which didn't happen too many times when he was in charge! We kept losing wickets just when partnerships were being formed and were in deathly trouble at 158 for 8. I had batted a long time for 46 but was true to my personal promise of using the bat unless leaving it completely – it was an important turn-around psychologically and certainly helped my performance for the rest of the series.

Braces and Danny saw us past two hundred which was a magic effort, with both guys' fighting qualities really coming through.

A total of 230 wasn't great, but it allowed us to be competitive, where a score of 180 would have left us floundering. Paddles demonstrated his class in netting six for and actually giving us a two-run lead. Only Srikkanth with a breezy 90 got the better of Paddles and it was good to see Braces running into form, picking up Azharuddin and Vengsarkar.

Ravi Shastri, who is a super bloke, was far from the darling of the crowds in that series. Taking strike against Chats, he pulled away and ambled down to the far end of the ground. When he got there he started waving his bat in the direction of the stand, obviously giving someone a mouthful. It turned out someone in the crowd was shining a mirror in his eyes as he was batting! It made us wonder what we were in for.

After a good partnership between Shake and Jonesy, Jonesy and I kicked on and we were nicely placed at 149 for 2. Rather like the first innings it turned to custard from there with six wickets falling for 30-odd and only Smith and Bracewell left. Danny had gone up the list to be night-watchman but unfortunately picked up another of the ducks that would later see him to a world record.

It was do-or-die stuff on day four and with Smithy, the nimble footed natural, and Braces hewing away at their spinners we got to 279. Chats stuck around for an hour and got two not out defending with his inimitable technique. We at least had something to bowl at and the gutsy performance from the tail had us hitting the field positive and ready to rip in.

The Indian crowd thought they were about to witness another victory for the home side and 40,000 streamed into the ground – a big noisy crowd which made for a terrific atmosphere.

First ball the great fast bowler had Srikkanth and not long after Braces picked up Sidhu and Vengsarkar – 50 for 3 and we were well into them. Smithy dived to catch Shastri and only Azza and Kapil were left. Only Azza and Kapil! They'd put on 50 and Kapil was going at a run a ball when he hammered Braces to mid wicket and Shake pulled in a screamer – he was beside himself and we swamped him like an Italian soccer team when the long haired guy nets one. Stumps were drawn with India 137-7, Ruds having picked up Azza in close off Braces to finish a remarkable afternoon.

The bad news was that the following day was a holy day and therefore the rest day. The good news was that our beer had arrived, and with a day off ahead of us we gave it a huge nudge. We invited the media and our supporters into the team room and had a great night. It was interesting seeing Don Cameron having a long chat with Braces about his performances on tour. Don had suggested after the first test that Braces might have been lucky to play in the match. Braces, with two fine innings and four second innings wickets to his name, was inviting Don to revise his opinion!

When play resumed, Braces bowled More early and Hadlee swept Patel aside to give him a pair in his first test. The arrival of Narendra Hirwani at the crease worried no-one and he soon finished it, spooning Braces to Chats down at square leg. Stumps were going everywhere and the match was over by 10 o'clock on the last day.

Thankfully we hadn't liquidated the beer ration totally and we celebrated hard. It was an amazing win, given the stuffing we had received in the first test and all the other things that make competing on the sub-continent so hard. Braces had a blinder, but everyone had chipped in with vital runs or catches at key times.

We went to Hyderabad feeling great and after winning the toss again decided to repeat the winning formula from Bombay, by taking first turn at bat. Things were looking a bit dire at 90 for 6 but Stockley was in great form throughout the series and we began to build a big partnership together. We got through to 220 at stumps and felt that another hour or so in the morning would set us up for a competitive first innings total. Stockley whistled a loosener from Kapil straight to Srikkanth at square leg after we'd added just one and we were back in trouble. He'd hit it like a dart, too, which was doubly frustrating. There was no repeat of the Bracewell heroics and I was left high and dry on 90.

Missing my hundred was one thing, but we also felt

that 250 wasn't enough on the Hyderabad wicket. We grafted pretty hard but they kept putting partnerships together and we eventually faced a deficit of a hundred. The second innings was probably our worst batting performance of the tour, and only Shake got a decent score, gutsing it to the end.

The collapse further underlined our brittleness at five, six and seven, even allowing for illness during the first test. We would have been lucky to get a hundred and fifty from those three spots in 18 innings, which makes big team totals pretty hard to come by. The bowlers had toiled hard but Paddles was virtually down to one leg by the end of the tour.

The one-day series involved five matches in ten days spread across 10,000 miles. It was travel, play, travel, play and although we were competitive in a couple of games our best result was the wash-out in game five. We played the second match in a half-built stadium, which was an interesting experience. In the fourth (and what was to prove the last) match, we finally ran into some form and knocked up 278-3. I was feeling pretty happy with myself, having scored 84 off 67 balls which I thought was a pretty impressive strike rate. Impressive, that is, until Azza got going and scored 108 off 65 – compared to him I was Geoffrey Boycott.

The last match was in Jammu, up in the north of India and a chillingly cold place. The weather closed in and we were due to leave the next day, the 20th of December, in order to be home in time for Christmas. There was a bit of tension about but thankfully the fog lifted and we let out a collective "you beauty" as we left the tarmac.

The tour had been memorable, but statistically unsuccessful. Statistics however, can never measure the spirit in the side, the feeling of triumph in Bombay and the courage displayed in Bangalore. Wrighty was a brilliant skipper – not just through any great tactical calls, but more because he was tough, he refused to lie down, and he taught me a lot about what it takes to succeed in test cricket. The Indians for their part were tough to play but were gentlemen off the field and the series was played in good spirit. The umpires had their moments as they always seem to, but at the end of the day Ayub and Hirwani were the real difference between the two sides.

It was to be seven years before I would take strike in Rajkot again . . .

Two Days, Three Figures, No Glory

The domestic summer of 1989/90 was a relatively quiet one for me, performing adequately against the touring Indians and having an unhappy time in the tri-series, where Rackemann extracted a fair measure of revenge for Perth by picking me up twice for blongers. The season was memorable for two great moments in cricket; Richard Hadlee picking up his 400th wicket in test cricket and Ian Smith donging the Indians around Eden Park on his way to 173.

It was one of the privileges of playing with Richard Hadlee that you were often there when history was made, but in true Hadlee fashion the joy for him was internal and it was business as usual for the rest of the match. The man who made the biggest fuss was businessman and long-time friend of New Zealand cricket Roger Bhatnagar, who strolled on to the field with 400 roses! Bung those in water thanks twelfthy.

Of course, Stockley's innings was just pure Stockley – team in the crap, Indians on fire and the little wicket keeper playing like a man on a beer for every boundary. Poor old Wassan went for 24 off one over, understanding too late that the ball on Stockley's pads is buffet bowling – help yourself.

Later that year we were off to England, on what is known as the tour of tours – to the home of cricket, where the facilities are great, the food is fine and the ale . . . well, there are plenty of places for a pint if you are that way inclined.

We had the nucleus of a strong side with many players having toured England previously and Wrighty and Paddles on their fourth and fifth trips respectively. I was dead keen to play in England as an international player after having played so many years of league cricket in the north of England. I had built up strong friendships with many people in England and I was looking forward to playing in front of them again, but this time on the international stage.

It was my chance to play on the famous grounds of England and in particular at the home of cricket, Lord's Cricket Ground in London. It was also widely known that this was to be Richard Hadlee's last cricket for his country, and Paddles being Paddles we knew that he would sign off in style.

During the Lord's test he was knighted for his services to the game and although the tour was not notable for too many Hadlee heroics, just being there for that was a rare experience. Of course, he didn't let anyone down in terms of his exit, picking up a wicket and with it a five wicket bag with his final delivery in test cricket.

The tour began with the traditional opener against the Duchess of Norfolk's XI and after I got out I thought it might be a good idea to have a little scout around the castle and soak up a bit of history. I'd made it over a couple of locked gates (which seemed a little inhospitable) and was just strolling up to the moat when a uniformed guy accompanied by a pack of savage-looking dogs suggested that I might like to have another go during visiting hours and that I was in fact trespassing on private property. The dogs didn't seem too amenable to debate so I bailed out pretty quickly!

We were playing an attractive brand of cricket on the tour, helped along by the Tetley Bitter sponsorship which provided a cash incentive for victories in the county matches. Because the counties were similarly motivated there were some excellent games of cricket, but it did mean the middle-order guys were looking to smash it more often than they were looking to build an innings. Regardless of the pros and cons of our build-up, we were in good shape for the first international cricket of the tour at Headingly in Leeds.

Headingly is a wonderful old ground and like the Basin is one of those arenas you can wander all the way around and still watch the cricket. I had actually played at the ground in my first game of league cricket but didn't get to bat as, lo and behold, Hogan batted through to win us the match.

To be back in front of my Yorkshire mates, who had just about set a record by getting me to secure thirty complimentaries for them, was exciting, particularly as I knew where they would be in the ground and that they would get progressively louder as the Tetley's set in.

Chris Pringle turned up at the ground looking for a few tickets and before long was throwing on a sleeveless with a fern on the front and running in to Gooch and Gower. Injuries to Sneds in particular had left us glaringly short in the seamers and Pring charged in and took his chance in typical fashion, dismissing Gooch for a memorable first scalp in international cricket.

It was a beautiful day and we made a good start, dismissing Gower early. Robin Smith wandered in next, swinging his 3lb bat like a wand, the little four-leaf clover on the back bringing him some early luck but thereafter he just murdered us. Later in the knock he began flat batting it over point and cover, which I was happy to observe from the mid wicket boundary! Paddles went from 9 overs 1 for 18 to 10 overs 2 for 26 and finished with 11 overs 2 for 45, seemingly a killer blow at the end of the innings.

One of the quirks of one-day internationals in England is that they are 55-over affairs, which means you have lunch midway through the first innings and only a ten minute break between innings. With England making 295, thanks largely to Smith's 120-odd demolition, we had little time to re-group between innings, but we were conscious of the need for a good start (no kidding) but also that if we did get a good start then victory was possible. It was a superb wicket and a rapid outfield so if we got the momentum up we had a real chance.

Wrighty and Jed got us away superbly and with the Poms shelling a few catches they had ninety-odd up in good time, below the required rate but with wickets in hand. Jones was out first and when Wrighty smashed one to gully just before tea I was on my way out with the rate having hopped up to six-odd. On the walk to the middle I wandered past Gower. He had his hands in his pockets and gave me a funny "who is this guy?" type of look – it was clear he didn't consider me the greatest threat in the world and I just about confirmed his suspicion when I inside-edged Hemmings just past leg stump to get off the mark.

After a couple more jittery moments, including a missed half chance to Allan Lamb, Hogan and I began to pick up runs reasonably comfortably. The boundaries were coming in most overs which made six an over not unattainable. Of course, batting with Hogan you're not going to miss many singles and he'll make the most of outfield shots. At one stage I was actually outscoring Hogan and that hasn't happened too often!

At 224 for two, with 72 required in 12 overs, Lewis bowled an over that turned the game on its head. First he had Crowe caught behind trying to pull and then two balls later Rutherford got a shocker of an LB and we went from a solid position to a perilous one. Paddles ambled out and smote one sizzling four but at 254 he was on his way with 42 still needed off five. I was still nudging away at the bowling but when Priest was out to a miracle catch by Gower at short mid-wicket things were looking dicey again, now 37 needed off four.

Ian Smith was next in and with Pringle, Morrison and Millmow left in the hut we were going to have to get a heck of a lot closer if the game was to be ours. With 27 needed from 17 balls, Gladstone Small bowled me a couple of loose ones and I got them both to the fence – 19 needed off 15. A few singles and the odd leg-bye and it was 13 needed off eight. Their Pringle bowled Stocks a full bunger on leg and he smashed it to the fence. I remember going down and saying "Keep boofing it Stocks" – I was pretty poked and it was great to see runs coming from the other end.

With nine needed off seven he picked up another run and was facing with eight needed off the last – De Freitas to bowl and me sitting up the other end on 99. First ball he had a flay at one and picked out Eddie Hemmings in the deep – super bloke Eddie but Michael Johnson he ain't so we scampered through for three. Five needed off five and we felt we were home but obviously getting out would have put huge pressure on anyone fresh.

De Freitas came in and dropped one on my legs – away it went through square and we needed three off four. I also had my hundred, a real buzz in front of my "other" home crowd. I don't recall getting many cheers throughout the knock but they were generous in their applause at three figures. The next ball De Freitas bowled me a bouncer which I was sure was a no-ball and told umpire Plews in no uncertain terms. Thankfully he took it in his stride and realised I was just fired up and desperate for a win – he was very much in control of a pumped-up young Kiwi. At three off three a dot ball the last thing we needed.

We decided to run the next one regardless but as it rolled down the wicket to the bowler I started the "Oh Shit Shuffle" before haring down the pitch. Stocks probably wasn't in the frame as the ball shaved the stumps and went through to Russell – two from two. Stockley on strike, the field up and he slammed it over mid off for four and victory.

An impromptu high five in mid-pitch followed, before we raced off arm in arm, a great victory achieved and the team standing on the balcony clapping us all the way off. It was the highest second innings chase to win a match in the history of the game and all the boys had pitched in to get us home. I still remember Richard Hadlee extending his hand and saying, "Well played Mark" – from Paddles a real accolade, and typical of his business-like approach to the game; no frills, no fuss.

I knew a few with the Yorkshire boys was on the cards that night and with a four-hour trip to London the next day I insisted on a good rub from Plums to make sure no stiffness set in. The match at the Oval was just two days away so moderation was certainly the order of the night.

It was also my first turn at the Oval and the uncharacteristically dry English summer had left the ground with a super-fast outfield and an even faster wicket. The pitch was a shiny white colour and any batsman will tell you that the combination of an ivory wicket and ebony bowlers is an extremely unattractive proposition. Devon Malcolm was lightning that day and Ken Rutherford can tell you all about Chris Lewis – that *was* a quick nut!

It all resulted in a very slow start and when Martin Crowe was dismissed in bizarre circumstances we were really struggling. Lewis bowled him one which climbed as it went past him and Russell caught it and just handed it to slip without appealing. Unfortunately, Hogan had started to stroll off and by the time he turned around the penny had dropped with the umpire and that was that.

Fifty-four for three wasn't the end of the world but we'd used up a fair amount of time and needed to move things along.

When the third ball to Rudders rose from nowhere he hardly moved before it smacked into his forehead. I ran down to hear him say something like "I'm not too good here" to which I replied "Yeah, there's a bit of claret about." Not exactly Harley Street diagnoses but we both knew that his day was over.

Paddles was not in the mood to get peppered by these

guys and hung round for a while before he too got a flyer which broke a bone in his hand.

At lunch we had three back in the pavilion and two in Ward 23, which wasn't a great state of affairs, but Priesty was keen to fight hard and we put on a hundred before he made way for my partner from Headingly, Smithy, who tried hard to get us up to a reasonable total.

Comparisons with the Michelin man are more often than not offensive, but having viewed the carnage I think he had gathered every piece of padding he could find and had popped the full grill on for good measure. I kept on collecting and pushed one wide of Allan Lamb to bring up my second hundred in three days. It was personally very satisfying but I felt we were a few short in such a run-conducive environment.

After a little chat with umpire Plews up in Yorkshire I also got involved with umpire Constant in London. I got the feeling his interpretation of what constituted a wide was very liberal in favour of the bowlers and asked him to clarify some of his rulings. His response, which on reflection was probably the right one, was simply to say "Just bat", which didn't help my mood any. In the end I got out gliding one off my face down to Robin Smith at third man (indicative of the carry) which in Australia would have had a fair chance of being wided.

In the break I went and saw Constant and apologised for my actions and he said he appreciated the apology and was happy to leave the matter there. I was astonished at the end of the game to hear that he had cited me for my behaviour! I was disappointed but delighted that team management dealt with me fairly and were not too officious in collecting the fine they had imposed on me.

I'm a firm believer in allowing officials to do their job and that players should afford them the respect they deserve but I can't stand umpires who think they should play bigger roles in the game than the players. Confident umpires who officiate to a very high standard, but who also communicate well with the players, are vital to the game because they ensure codes of conduct are maintained but also that the players can enjoy a bit of banter without discovering they are all queuing outside the match referee's office after the match for the mildest indiscretion.

The England side made a shaky start but, thanks to M. Greatbatch grassing centurion Gooch early on, they recovered and eventually achieved a comfortable victory. What hurt more was that by virtue of a higher overall run rate they also took out the Texaco Trophy. My two hundreds had pretty much been in vain, but it was still very satisfying to reflect on a great victory at Headingly.

Light the Touchpaper

Walking around Eden Park at the end of the semi-final, many of the guys in tears and the crowd standing and cheering as if we had won, I had an unbelievable emptiness inside. In the first game against Australia just a month earlier the ground had been half-full, a reflection of the team's pretty miserable summer. I couldn't even make the side which shows what sort of form I was in.

Now we were saluted as heroes but the inescapable fact remained – the great month was over and everything we had built up for had been snatched away. It was like coming home from a holiday and finding your house ransacked – there were all these How? and Why? questions. But the only criminals that day were the light-fingered fraudster Miandad and the smash and grab burglar Inzamam. The nation had got behind us and the team had given cricket a huge lift, but the ride was over and it was time to get off.

When the team assembled at the Devonport Naval Base in 1990 before the tour of Pakistan, the goals for the eighteen months leading up to the World Cup were spelled out. Sure, we didn't accomplish all of those goals, but Wally and Martin had put a great deal of thought and planning into the programme and at least we had a path to follow.

In the spring of 1991 a group of established players teamed up with some fringe contenders and headed to South Australia for pre-season matches. Again, we didn't win all our games but played a good standard of cricket and it was an excellent way to get us in the groove for the coming summer. We actually got a bit of a stuffing at the hands of the Academy but playing and training in good conditions were more important than game by game success.

A couple of the guys might have been lucky to get to the Cup at all after a frightening incident on the way back from training. We had two vans and the first to leave took off with Chris Cairns at the wheel. There was a little bit of erratic lane changing on the motorway and as a car of hoons revved past Cairnsy gave them a wave, which I think they must have misinterpreted as an unfriendly gesture.

When the boys turned into the hotel they were mortified to see the hoons follow them into the car park. They (the hoons, of course) leaped out of the car armed with baseball bats and it looked like there was going to be a bit of damage incurred but thankfully the situation was quickly diffused with only Chris Pringle (who had grabbed the window seat) getting a blow through the window. Scary stuff, and the last thing you'd expect in downtown Adelaide! Thankfully, that was the only serious threat to life and limb and we returned home keen to get into the Shell Trophy before the arrival of the England team early in 1992.

I got off to a reasonable start in the Trophy and things were looking good for the summer until 1992 dawned. It was if the guy who doled out the run vouchers just said "Sorry Pads, you've had your ration."

I couldn't get a run for Central Districts and missed out in the one-dayer against England, so counted myself fortunate to make the side for the first test at Lancaster Park. I missed out twice there and was promptly dropped. Robin Smith picked me up at short point off the full face of the pad. I didn't get near it and tell the story not to seek sympathy but as a good illustration of how when it's not rolling for you then the breaks just don't happen. Thankfully, the sporting wheel of fortune was about to roll around but for the moment the selectors had me planted firmly on "miss a turn".

I wasn't actually that keen on a game of hit and giggle when Franko phoned and asked me to take part in a six-a-side tournament as part of his benefit. Franko had been such a good supporter of mine over many years and I knew not fronting would be contrary to our friendship, regardless of how ratshit I was feeling.

I threw some kit together and arrived at the ground only to realise I'd left my bat at home. Chris Gott, a Yorkshireman who was playing with the Ellerslie club for the English winter, was taking part and I had just jacked him up a contract with Stuart Surridge. I rifled through his kit and grabbed a bat, asking if I could borrow it for the day. It felt good in my hands and before too long I was boofing it everywhere for some of Franko's corporate supporters – it felt bloody good just to hit a few in the middle again!

At the end of the day Gotty came up and asked for the bat back but I wasn't letting that one go and had to spend some time convincing him that I would get him a replacement as soon as possible. It was that bat which helped me get the side off to flyers in the World Cup.

While I felt I was in the top fourteen players in the country, my form was far from special and it was with some relief that I heard my name called out. World Cups on home soil are once in a lifetime affairs for most players and I would have been shattered to have missed out. A couple of one-dayers against England were our final preparation and I missed out twice as we crashed in both games. The team was not winning and I was not playing well – not the best way to kick off a World Cup campaign.

Before the Cup began all the teams flew to Sydney for

the official launch and numerous other public relations and marketing commitments. At the rather lavish launch dinner we were treated to a keynote speaker from England who decided a running gag putting down New Zealand and Australia would have the crowd in stitches. Unfortunately, he missed the mark and the players were infuriated.

Many of the English guys were embarrassed at his performance but their embarrassment turned to anger as a female impersonator came on and started sending up the Queen. Botham and a few of his teammates actually got up and walked out, which is a reasonable indication of the tenor of his remarks.

The dinner aside, we had a great couple of days in Sydney and returned to New Zealand keen to start the World Cup in style, by beating Australia. We had a well-balanced side but Murphy Sua was an interesting selection, given his relative lack of experience at international level. You can count on the fingers of one hand the successful left arm seamers in international one-day cricket and Murphy when selected for the World Cup had played just two Shell Cup games. It was a credit to him that he stayed high-spirited throughout the tournament when it was pretty obvious that only injury would get him on the park.

I had just read the outstanding story of John Bertrand's 1983 America's Cup challenge and was impressed with his technique of neutralising the potentially huge psychological barrier of taking the cup away from American waters. At that stage it had never been done, so rather than think about the opposition as *Liberty* or Dennis Conner's crew, they just referred to "the red boat". It was a technique which I thought translated nicely into what we were trying to achieve so I shared the idea with Hogan, who was immediately behind it. As a team starting as underdogs it was better to think about colours than Australia and Dean Jones or the West Indies with Richie Richardson. Reducing them to flesh and blood individuals in different colours turned out to be an excellent way of diluting the mental pressure.

Standing out on Eden Park with the anthem playing I was filled with anticipation but disappointed I would not be making an on-field contribution. If sports betting were around in those days the odds on a New Zealand victory would have been long, and would have grown longer after Wrighty was bowled by McDermott and Jones got a shocking leg before from umpire Hayat – we thought it was a bit on the nose to have to suffer dodgy decisions from Hayat on our own deck!

Despite these setbacks the dressing room remained very positive, which was a good sign for the tournament. Crowe and Rutherford played superbly and set up a defendable target on a pitch which would suit our mediums as the day wore on. A superb bowling and fielding display and a handy benefit of the doubt decision to get rid of Dean Jones and the boys were home – we had knocked over the world champions. It was remarkable how the ground filled up during the day and there was a real buzz in the ground by the time Jonesy caught Reid in the deep.

Only Wrighty and Jones of the batsmen had missed out and as I was not considered as a top-three player at that stage the batting line-up remained the same for the next outing against Sri Lanka (to us, the blue team). In the process of bowling the Sris out, Wrighty fell heavily on his shoulder and although he went out and made fifty it was clear he was struggling and I knew I had a chance to make the side for the South African match. I was keen to play, obviously, but there was time for Plums to weave some magic on Wrighty's shoulder before the weekend.

That night I had an interesting experience in a hotel in Hamilton when a guy came up and suggested Jeff Crowe was far more worthy of a place in the side than I was. I had nothing against Chopper but this guy was one of those Cricket Society free-lunchers who buy you a beer when you're up and search for the hero du jour when you're down. It was a display I didn't need but if he was any barometer of public opinion I knew that if I made the side

I needed runs in large dollops to enjoy any sort of support. It's funny to think that at times I have actually been booed when I've walked on to New Zealand grounds wearing the silver fern – mind you, it was south of the Basin so I guess I wouldn't be the first to be a victim of that sort of parochialism.

Initially, Jones was mooted to open the dig but they decided the Jones, Crowe, Rutherford combination at three, four and five was working well and it would be foolish to change a successful formula. At the nets on Friday, Wrighty was declared unfit to play and Wally gave me the news that I was in the side and that I would open the batting. Wally wanted me to go out and be positive, to do what he thought I was best at – namely, hit the ball hard and often. It was not rocket science but at that stage it was just what I needed – nothing complicated, just get out and give it a nudge.

Yes, he did want us to make the most of the field being up in the first fifteen overs, but did not burden us with specific targets which so often are counter-productive and apply pressure when it needn't be there. In my own mind I was looking at it as a one-on-one confrontation and building myself up to grab the initiative. The fasties always like to intimidate, but this was my chance to give them something to think about and to let them know that I was having as much fun in the confrontation as they were.

All that would have to wait though as we had a bowl first and although Kirsten played superbly he got very little support from the guys around him and only a late flurry from McMillan gave their score any level of respectability.

As Roc and I wandered out to the middle I said to him, "I wouldn't mind having first hit today" – not the typical reaction to facing Allan Donald, accurately billed as the fastest white man in the world. It was indicative of my state of mind – pumped up and ready to go, knowing full well that a good start would turn their score from achievable to a stroll for the guys to follow. I had a bit of a look at Donald to start with but in McMillan's first over I had a boof at him and Gotty's Stuart Surridge put it over the fence. McMillan is an aggressive and able allrounder and he was none too pleased. He came down and said, "What the f— do you think you're doing!"

"Just get back and bowl pal," I replied. The gloves were off and we were into it!

McMillan was soon replaced by Snell who had the mortification of seeing one of my off drives fly over third man for six. A few balls later I got it right, though, and thumped him over long on for six more. The South Africans started to lose it a bit, particularly as Rod Latham was firing at the other end – we were going shot for shot against a pretty good attack.

In an attempt to mix it up a bit, Wessels brought on Kuiper who had played a bit for Derby and bowled little mediums. I was delighted to see something a little less rapid than Donald and Co and I realised I had a really good stick in my hands when a big shot over long on actually went on to the roof of the stand. By the end of the over Kuiper was struggling to let it go and he finished his spell after six balls for 18 runs.

By now the old heart was racing and I had to take a spell. When I sank to my knees, Rod came down to check up on me. I was dizzy and just needed a moment to get it together, but the crowd were going bananas and I just wanted to whack everything. It was fitting that I got out to Kirsten trying to hit him into Royal Terrace and by the end of the knock I was pretty jaded, which is a bit odd given that I'd only been out there for an hour and a bit and faced only 60 balls.

I got back to the dressing room, took my kit off and before I knew it I was down by the coffin having half an hour's kip! It's not something I've done before or since and I think it just reflected how much the knock had taken it out of me emotionally . . . I'd like to think the body could handle 60 deliveries before packing it in!

Zimbabwe was an interesting challenge for the team as

again a game of cricket broke the drought in Hawke's Bay. It was a case of McLean in the Rain but the Zimbabwe guys were very good to us in the way they remained keen to play without putting undue pressure on the umpires for a cessation in proceedings.

Some magic from Hogan and a super knock from Jonesy gave us a good total and although Cairnsy had some trouble early on we moved through our overs quickly and made sure that the weather wasn't going to deny us. Zimbabwe was a must win and anything less than two points against them would put extra pressure on to beat someone else. With the win in the bank only the West Indies stood between the unrated Kiwis and a spot in the semis.

By now public support had returned and a big crowd transformed the terraces into a collage of DB signs, sun hats and flying debris. A bit of that debris upset Winston Benjamin for by the time the Windies took the field the foam cups had been drained and filled frequently and it was "anything goes" down on the fence.

Looking back at the scoresheet, a side with Lara, Richardson and Haynes would be a match for anyone but context presents a more realistic view. Lara had yet to really arrive on the international stage, Richardson was badly out of nick and Haynes was in the twilight of his career.

Hogan won the toss and sent them in, with Dipak immediately dropping on to a length and keeping them pinned – his 10 overs for 19 was one of the best bowling performances of the tournament. When Hooper tried to break the shackles he hit what Don Cameron described in the *Herald* as "possibly one of the highest catches ever seen at Eden Park". Unfortunately, I found myself underneath it and was very relieved to drag it in, particularly as I was right in front of the terraces at the time and I'm sure would have earned plenty of stick if I'd shelled it.

The Windies ended up on 203 which doesn't sound like a lot but with Ambrose and Marshall charging in can be made to seem like an awful lot more.

I was keen to use the same approach as I'd used against South Africa, though, and refused to be intimidated. Well, I refused to *look* intimidated anyway, because they made a couple of comments out there which got me thinking a bit! I took first strike at Ambrose and found it difficult to get him away at first but soon speared one low over point for four to get things moving. It didn't go very high but Logie was fielding there and it was too elevated for little Gus.

After a while I thought I'd better get down to Curtly and try and whistle him over the top but didn't get bat on it. As I turned around and went back to prepare for the next ball I became aware of a large shadow over the batting crease. I thought at first a cloud had passed over the sun but it turned out to be Curtly, who said quietly, "If you do that again I'll run through man" – meaning he would deliver well past the crease. I was finding him pretty rapid at 22 yards so I wasn't relishing the prospect of facing him off 16.

Haynes was fielding in the covers and was having plenty to say to Rod and me so I was determined to shut him up.

Marshall came in and I played what would be one of the best shots I think I've ever played. It just seemed to drop into the slot as I charged down and hit him into the Western stand. Marshall was less enthused and screamed, "Greatbatch, if you do that again I will kill you man" – a remark for which I didn't have a ready response and I certainly wasn't going to get into verbals with Marshall. I did ask Haynes what he thought and he quietened down for a bit. I got out to Benjamin in the end and although a few of the guys struggled to get started, the skipper played magnificently and saw us home.

Five from five and we were in to the semis! There was never any question of easing off, though, as we wanted to stay with the winning habit and maintain the momentum, not only within the side but also the burgeoning public support which had escalated with every win. Wally was a little worried about a trip to the 'Brook because of the predominance of scarfies in the area and the keenness of the team to sample some of the hospitality in the Cook or the Gardies. He needn't have worried though as we were as keen as he was to be six and six after India.

It was bitterly cold in Dunedin – long sleevers, long johns and, for the Indians, long faces. They hated the cold conditions and in the end played like it. Azharuddin said in the pre-match interview "it's like at playing at Derby" which Wrighty confirmed with a shiver. Having said that they did manage 230 but the boundaries are pretty small sideways in Dunedin so it was about a 210 on most grounds.

Rod and I got things going again and with a strong wind blowing you could choose the end to have a flay from. I got it wrong at one stage and had a big mow at Kapil which went high in the air. The wind was so strong that the ball actually started coming back towards me and turned a high but comfortable catch to an embarrassing nightmare for poor Sanjay Manjrekar. I don't think he got a finger on it in the end. I was starting to get dropped a bit but I figured if I hit it hard it was going to take some catching and there was no point curbing my style at this stage of the competition. We all managed to chip in with a few and got home quite comfortably in the end.

During the tournament we had organised a number of bats to be signed by the other teams as a great souvenir for the players but also for fund-raising activities in the future. All the teams had obliged up to this point and the Indians seemed to see no problem either. The only difficulty came when we went to collect our bats and discovered that there were twenty fewer than had been sent in! Naturally, we were a bit upset but the Council didn't want a major incident and let the matter rest. Maybe the Indians used the bats as firewood in an attempt to heat their dressing room but no-one saw any ash about.

What could have been a blight on the night was soon forgotten as we all headed off to the Cook for a celebratory ale – the least we could do for the brave lads who had resisted the elements on the terraces for the day. We were

Century up but no celebration – Perth 1989.

Visual Impact/Richard Hare

How's that bet looking Both? – v England at the Basin.

I.G. Blackwell

Square cutting Ambrose – in the air but too high for Gus Logie.

Fifty v the Windies – a great feeling.

J.G. Blackwell

Partner in crime – Rod Latham.

Visual Impact/Richard Hare

When I lose it, I really lose it!

Comparing dodgy fingers with Stockley.

Batting with Hogan at Pukekura – cricketing heaven.

J.G. Blackwell

Stand and deliver – Kuiper goes on the roof.

in the mood for celebration and Wrighty soon settled back in to his old scarfie habits and ended up leading the boys on a compulsory karaoke.

The real benchmark for our improvement came at the Basin where we were due to play an England side which had stuffed us out of sight in both tests and one-dayers only a month before. They were keen to win because it gave them the opportunity to lead the round robin and play the first semi-final on the Saturday. With an old side and some injuries lingering they were keen to rest up for as many days as possible before the final.

We were training really effectively now and having short, sharp sessions rather than endless nets – everything we did had a purpose. After one practice Botham wandered past me and suggested we have a wager on who could hit the biggest six the next day. Word was obviously getting around about our tactics and it was flattering that one of the game's greats was bothering to take me on in such a competition. What he didn't do was invite me for a trip in the helicopter that he, Lamb and Smith had hired to take them over to the Cloudy Bay vineyard for a tasting. Plenty of style, those lads!

Chris Doig sang the National Anthem and we took the field feeling light years away in terms of confidence from our last encounter.

Dipak cleaned up Botham early which made the wager pretty safe and while Hick and Smith batted really well they took the pressure off just when the foot should have been going on our throats. Jed bowled really well at the death and we restricted them to around 200, which we were confident about chasing given our performances to date. Smithy actually picked up a migraine so I had to don the keeping kit and I'm sure I made an incongruous sight in his gear, with the pads only just reaching my knees. I was happy to pick up a catch, though, and just missed a brace when I missed a diving chance off Harris.

We got away to a good start but I rifled one down to

De Freitas who picked it up at full stretch right on the line. I'd earlier landed one just nearby so my dismissal may not have seemed too bright, but I had licence to go for it and had to keep playing that way.

The win, with Hogan guiding us home again, was a huge morale booster and it was good to beat a side that had been playing well and had beaten many of the top sides comfortably. The England team were full of many of the big names of world cricket and although some of them had played better cricket in earlier years it was still a high calibre scalp.

Botham settled the wager in what the tabloids might consider typical style. A group of us wandered into the English dressing room for a chat and sitting in the middle of the floor was a case of Cloudy Bay Sauvignon. It was a very refreshing way to finish up, but Botham suggested no-one leave until there was nothing left – lucky plenty of us went in! The win also meant we had beaten every team we might meet in the semi-finals apart from our final round robin opponents, Pakistan.

The Pakis had started to lift their game after some poor form early on – they had all the players but hadn't seem to gel as a unit, something of a trait in Pakistan cricket. That all changed at Lancaster Park as they came out steaming knowing that only a win would give them any chance of a semi-finals berth.

There was plenty of media speculation about us possibly throwing the game in order to gain a home ground advantage for the semi, but that was nonsense as there was no way we wanted to break the momentum in any way. It seemed the news of our success hadn't made it to Christchurch as only 11,000 turned up – it was a midweek game so maybe they save their sick grandmother excuses for the footie season – a pretty poor effort and guys like Harris, Cairns and Latham deserved more.

With seven players not making double figures I was forced to try to anchor it a bit and only Gavin Larsen and extras made much of a contribution. I got snared by Mushtaq sweeping and with an inadequate total and a Ramiz century the game was over and so was our winning run. With the Windies missing out across the Tasman it was off to Eden Park for a re-match with the side that had just humbled us. Although we took some lessons from the game we tried not to get too upset by the whole thing. It was considered more of an aberration and we felt confident about turning the tables as we left for Auckland.

We warmed up on the main oval which is not always customary and it was great to see so many people streaming into the ground.

Hogan won the toss and we had a bat in perfect conditions. I managed to get a couple over the ropes but probably got a bit carried away and ended up making a mess of a slower one from Aaqib. It was clear he hadn't enjoyed being hit for six as my dismissal was greeted with a barrage of abuse. Despite the Pakistani accent he was using words I was more than familiar with!

We looked like we might be in a bit of trouble at 80-odd for three but then our innings became the Crowe show and he played one of the greatest knocks I've ever seen, particularly when you think about who was bowling. Rudders was brilliant in support and between them they set up a score that was going to be competitive against any side, especially with our bowlers in good form and our field placings accurate.

My role in the innings didn't finish with my dismissal but I wish it had. I ended up running for Hogan after he'd pulled his hamstring; not an easy task, all the noise making communication difficult. We seemed to have it sorted out well and Hogan was on his way to another ton when Stockley and I had a shocking mix-up and Hogan was gone. I just couldn't hear and trying to run on sight isn't in the manual. Even with this setback a score of 250-plus was always going to be demanding and we lunched confidently, but aware of the task ahead.

Pakistan began quite well but we picked up a couple of wickets and really put the screws on, to the point where they needed 140 from the last 20 with eight wickets left. When they lost Imran and Malik in quick succession the rate hadn't changed but now they had only six wickets left. A big guy who hadn't had much of a Cup came out to join Miandad, who was just pottering about, collecting his ones and generally being very inoffensive.

Now came the smash and grab act which, by the look of the guy, he'd already tried on a bakery. It was an astonishing knock and one that we are unlikely to see again, particularly in such a pressure situation. Wrighty has taken a bit of stick for his captaincy that day, but there were plenty of us out there who had been around at this level of cricket long enough to say, "Hey, this doesn't look quite right." We didn't and that's that.

The fraudster Miandad used all the experience he'd gained over five World Cups, feeding the strike to Inzamam who just kept smashing it. There were some shots that defied explanation and it was all so clean. Although Miandad seemed to be out there a long time for not many he actually ended with nearly a run a ball and guided them home expertly. Even though they still had a bit of work to do when Inzamam was out, until we had Miandad the game was always alive.

After the emotional farewell to the crowd, the dressing room was a pretty empty old place but we soon picked ourselves up and reflected on a month that few would have predicted.

For most of that team there won't be another home World Cup, but to come from nowhere to be competitive in a semi-final against the eventual champions demonstrated a number of things. We were well organised and well led and we all knew our roles, which is so important in developing spirit. We enjoyed fabulous support throughout the Cup and were soon playing for all of those great supporters rather than the previously nebulous "country" that had bagged us in February. We had some good fortune but also made our own luck by being positive in everything we did.

Above all, we had a spirit unmatched in any New Zealand side I've played in. There was none of the divisiveness that had punctuated a number of other sides I'd been involved in and we were all pulling for each other. It was a great little cricketing vignette which should have set the game up and gained a franchise in the minds of New Zealand sports fans. Unfortunately, the nuts were working loose and the wheels were about to come off.

Three Day Tour

Well, it was a little longer than that if you throw in the tour of Zimbabwe, but the Sri Lankan leg was over before it started as far as I was concerned. New Zealanders don't have to deal with bombs and I wasn't going to hang around and find out what the Tamils' next tactic would be. What I didn't realise at the time was the profound effect this act of terrorism was going to have on the team and on New Zealand cricket. Our hotel was not the only thing shaken to the rafters.

It was a team of very happy and very united cricketers who jumped on the plane for the tour of Zimbabwe and Sri Lanka. Only Cairns and Morrison, both on the injured list, and Wright, who'd declared himself unavailable, were missing from the World Cup squad and we were expecting to win well against Zimbabwe. We knew Sri Lanka would be difficult, with home conditions a factor, but high hopes of success there as well. I had toured Zimbabwe previously and was looking forward to catching up with the likes of Eddo Brandes, Ian Butchart and David Houghton, who had looked after the Young New Zealand side so well.

I was, in fact, accused of being too friendly with the opposition on that tour, which is pretty bizarre stuff.

They'd played very little test match cricket and after series with India and Pakistan actually remained unbeaten – a fact which they had emblazoned on a sign at Harare Sports Ground. In avoiding defeat against those two teams, Zimbabwe had demonstrated they not only had a fair amount of talent, but also that they were a determined and proud side. In spite of this we were confident we had the fire-power to notch up some wins.

I managed to get a ton early in the tour and was pleased to get to grips with the slow, low wicket at Bulawayo. In the first test they picked a number of medium pacers, who were not difficult on the slow track. I decided to boof it and ended up back in the hut by lunch with 87 off 79 balls.

Being caught on the boundary at long-off before lunch on the first day of a test is an unusual mode of dismissal, but I sensed the opportunity of a hundred before lunch, which not many have done. I could tell my captain was unhappy and my trotting out the "live by the sword, die by the sword" cliche did nothing to help his mood. There wasn't a great deal else to enthuse over, although Rod Latham did get his first test ton.

With a bit of rain about, it soon became clear that the equipment wasn't up to test match standard, with water getting under the covers, and the Zimbabweans were pretty negative. When they got onto the field they displayed little interest in the target we had set and the game petered out to a draw. I had finished the match with back-to-back eighties which, although satisfying, left me close to a couple of comfortable centuries. Ironically, I was out trying to give it a nudge in the second dig because I was running out of time before the declaration.

The second test at Harare was a much better game with Hogan playing magnificently for 140 and Dipak bowling them out on the last day, taking 6-50. It was satisfying to win and given that it was our first test win since 1990, and the first under Martin's captaincy, we were keen to celebrate. Martin was very hard on the Zimbabweans, almost to the extent of being over the top. They were a new nation and desperate to do well. In addition, their administrators were inexperienced in international cricket and appeared to Hogan to be very stubborn. I think he could have cut them some slack, and his action in taking down the sign which proclaimed their unbeaten status was unnecessary and demonstrated that he had got a little overzealous in his approach to the series.

The only sour note as far as most of the team were concerned was the racist remarks endured by Dipak and Murphy Sua. It seemed to be at its worst in the second one-dayer after an unfortunate dismissal.

The Flower brothers were running superbly between the wickets but it didn't take long before we realised it was more than just fraternal intuition that was getting them between the sticks so quickly. I was at mid wicket and Harry was at cover and we just couldn't run them out. Dipak noticed that they were a little quick out of the blocks and stopped before delivering with Grant Flower well out of his ground. Nothing seemed to change so he stopped a second time – still with no change in the Zimbabwean tactics. By now our patience was exhausted and when Flower was caught out of his ground a third time Dipak nipped the bails off.

Naturally, none of us wanted to get a wicket this way but the message was having a hard time getting through and they were just picking up singles at will. Dip's reception from then on was a disgrace, with racist taunts frequenting the afternoon. It certainly gave us an interesting insight into racial harmony in Zimbabwe. Thankfully, we picked up a win to give us a clean sweep of the one-dayers and a nice boost before we took off for Sri Lanka.

We had a big night's celebration after the game but when we prepared to leave early the next morning there was no sign of the skipper. I hammered on his door for some time and it was a shattering sight which greeted me when the door finally opened. A stark naked Crowe, clearly not a hundred percent, and his gear unpacked and all over the place. We managed to get a few things together but left a number of souvenirs of clothing behind as we hurried to the airport.

Having made it and checked in we settled down for a cup of coffee and a spot of breakfast and Hogan went off to the gents. We thought nothing more of it until the cleaner came out yelling "There's someone dead in the toilets maan, there's someone dead in the toilets." We sprinted in and there was Hogan, fast asleep in the corner, far from dead, but probably more dead than alive! It proved to be a very long flight to Colombo for one M.D. Crowe.

It was a long flight anyway and I sat next to the biggest man I have ever seen in my life. He was from one African tribe or another and I understood why the British were so terrified on *Zulu Dawn*. I tried to have a bit of a yarn but he didn't speak any English so my opportunity to get on his side was lost. Everything about him was big including his body odour, which is hard yakka in economy class.

We were all relieved to make it to Colombo and the armed guards on our bus made it clear we were in a land in turmoil. There was also a sinister-looking guy on the bus, obviously Secret Service or whatever the Sri Lankan equivalent is. After a day or so there and a couple of training runs at 8.30 in the morning, Wally suggested we start the following day a little later to get ourselves completely caught up on sleep and our bodies back in order. We were due to have a bus trip up to Kandy so there was no need to be up and away at the crack of dawn.

I was asleep when the bomb blew. I was rooming with Mark Haslam who was on his first tour and hadn't quite sorted out the appropriate frequency for trips to the laundry. His gear had something of a hum to it but that couldn't have woken me. My next thought was that a naval exercise was taking place in the harbour but soon teammates were running through my room and out to the balcony which overlooked the ocean and, more significantly, the road below. I joined them on the balcony and with no ships in view was attracted by a plume of black smoke coming from the beachfront road. We were shaken and confused but we soon realised it was a bomb – scary stuff.

I suggested to Has that we have a look and as we entered the lobby we could see that every pane of glass in the hotel had been shattered. Outside the hotel was a large iron gate, which we could see over quite comfortably. A huge hole dominated the scene and there was a black BMW on the side of the road which had been overturned by the blast.

A man in uniform was on the periphery and I asked him what was going on. His reply was curious: "This sort of thing happens all over the world, not just here." There was flesh on the ground; a sickening sight and one that I'd be happy never to have to experience again. Initially we were told a suicide bomber had driven up with a grenade in his hand; later it was revealed he'd been on a motorbike and strapped up with explosives. The lies had begun.

Whether it was gelignite or a double happy is not really significant but we were in no mood for having the story change halfway through about anything; we needed the truth if we were to make an informed decision about the future of the tour. To make matters worse it was Heroes week for the Tamils, during which they celebrate their martyrs. No-one could tell us what their next target might be in such a "celebration".

We met in Wally's room and started firing questions at a New Zealand government representative and our own team management. The government man was comparing it with a bomb going off in London, somewhat irrelevant in terms of our current well-being. I asked them whether they could guarantee our safety, which was a tough one to answer but at least they were upfront and offered no guarantee. Manager Leif Dearsley had phoned New Zealand Cricket and the first message back was that they would support the team in whatever decision they came to. This was comforting but unfortunately was soon to be proved another lie.

It was decided to meet that evening and vote as a team on whether or not the tour should continue. Eighteen of us were in the meeting but the votes came to nineteen. Unfortunately, the manager's wife had decided to pop in a vote so we had to have a recount.

After the votes were counted there was a nine-all split. Crowe and Jones were contracted and had no choice and Leif had new riding instructions so it soon became clear who was in the Stay camp and who was in the Leave camp. The leader of the Leaves was Ken Rutherford, who was vocal in his support for the tour to be abandoned – comments like "it's just like '87" and "it's just not safe here" remain clear in the memory.

Hogan said that the tour must be called off because we couldn't perform with nine guys missing, at which point Andrew Jones became annoyed on the basis that at nine-each there should be another vote. Before that vote took place the news went around that Peter McDermott was on his way over to resurrect the tour. It meant another few days hanging around the hotel – strolling around the streets had lost all appeal.

McDermott gathered the team and gave us the news that he wanted the tour to continue and that he was there to assess the situation and ensure that the team would be safe from then on. I thought it was strange that he wanted to address us individually as we were a team and surely should be dealt with as one. In the team meeting he said, "I will not put undue pressure on any individual," which I thought odd given that if the discussions were to be friendly, why did they need to be held in private.

Wally Lees was first in and had the acid put right on him, to the point where McDermott asked for his resignation if he continued with his desire to leave the tour. When I was summoned, McDermott's first words were, "I know I said I wouldn't pressure anyone, but I'm going to pressure you." He told me that I was important to the side but I couldn't help but feel he hadn't heard.

"The guys want to go home," I said. "There was a team vote taken and nine of us want to go home." He was having none of it.

I appreciate he was in an invidious position but I think some of his tactics were dubious. I wasn't in Sua's meeting but apparently it got pretty personal. Chris Harris had three meetings before finally being convinced to continue and was even unsure as the bus pulled into the lobby to take the remaining players off to a beach resort for a couple of days.

For my part I felt I should be loyal to the team decision and frankly I just didn't feel safe in that environment. I couldn't justify in my own mind why we should stay. As it happened, six of us came home, Willie Watson and I the only single players to return. This earned us both a bit of stick, which was unbelievable and showed a strange disregard for our family and friends.

The word soon got around that Rutherford had sold us out to secure himself a contract, which was a remarkable turnaround and typifies the inconsistency and self-justification of the guy. One minute it was not safe and we should be hauling arse out of there, the next it was OK because he was getting paid a bit more. Did he genuinely feel it was unsafe in the first place? Or was he going to keep his fingers crossed for the rest of the tour? He took money over personal conviction and his teammates, which was difficult to swallow at the time. I ran into him at a Bledisloe Cup game in 1995 and had a beer with him, but he's not the sort of guy you'd want batting for your life – unless, of course, he was only going to get paid if you lived!

The next to have a crack at changing my mind was Hogan. By now the tour was definitely going ahead and he was desperate to have as many established players with him as possible. I consider his action selfish and his lack of respect for my decision was not in keeping with our friendship. I've never had a problem with some of the younger guys wanting to stay because they may never have been given another shot but some guys made some compromises and at the end of the day showed themselves for what they really are.

We left the tour having been told that there would be no repercussions over our decision to leave. After the steady passage of lies and half-truths we had been exposed to in the previous few days, I took this with a grain of salt. I was reselected for the one-day series against Pakistan and felt they had been true to their word, but I was soon to discover that all was not forgiven.

When Hogan had pulled out of the test side with an infected finger, Wally and Don Neely agreed that I should captain the side. My name was put forward to the Board, which is the due process, but it ended up going to McDermott who clearly objected to my being in charge. My opportunity to captain New Zealand was gone and the Rutherford era had begun. Although Martin returned to captain the side, Rutherford became the likely successor from that point on.

Wally Lees remained in charge of the side and finished the season with cricket in great shape. We had only just missed winning the test against Pakistan, we had squared the series with Australia and we had lost a cliffhanger one-day series in the last over of the fifth match. The one-dayers had attracted great crowds and people were positive about cricket and voting with their wallets. It makes the sacking of Warren Lees bewildering to say the least.

When he inherited the side at the end of 1990 there were a number of seasoned players leaving the game. Wal had nurtured some new talent and refreshed some old and the side was playing well and, importantly, succeeding.

I can't accept that reasons other than Sri Lanka were a factor in his demise, which remains a great shame for New Zealand cricket, exacerbated by the fact that the man who was taking up the reins and leading us to a higher plane was none other than Geoff Howarth. Give me a break!

We had set off on the tour a happy unit and one that enjoyed being together. The bomb changed a lot of relationships because we failed to stick together and people chose themselves over the team. The loyalty we had shown each other during the World Cup seemed to have vanished and makes me question how close we were in reality. I hope a New Zealand side never has to deal with that sort of trauma again because, as the Greenpeace people assert, the long term effects of the fallout are very hard to quantify.

Up There For Thinking

And down there for dancing, as any discussion about the mental side of my game soon revolves around facing the quick boys who have certainly taught me a few new steps over the years. Cricket, more than just about any other game, requires intense concentration over long periods of time.

Other games require levels of concentration that are just as high, but seldom are they spread over five days – long days of which sometimes you are merely a constituent part rather than being integral to the goings on. You have to stay sharp, though, because if you're on another planet when Mark Taylor hits one in the air for the first time in a day and a half you'll find out on re-entry that there won't be another chance.

As alluded to, my mental hurdles have been largely about handling quick bowling, which may seem strange when my record shows I batted for ten hours at Perth – one of the quickest tracks around. The quicks I'm talking about are in another class, at times freakish, and while I'm not going to start trotting out lines like "be afraid, be very afraid" these guys have had a profound effect on my career.

We headed to Pakistan in late 1990 with a new coach, a new captain and a number of new players. We were aware that Pakistan is a difficult place to tour but felt good together as a team and were keen to take the Pakis on. I managed to pick up a hundred early in the tour and was looking forward to the test matches.

In the first test, at Karachi, Rudders and I had put on a few and although Akram and Younis were demanding we felt they were tiring and that we had a chance to push on and post a reasonable first innings tally. Unfortunately, we were both out in quick succession, me pushing one back off Ijaz Ahmed, who bowled little left arm slingers. The two Ws did the rest and dominated the remainder of the match, which we lost by an innings.

I was badly sawn off in the second dig and had my first experience of Pakistan umpires in full flight. While I'm not too keen on becoming Salman Rushdie's flatmate, I'd have to say that if they weren't cheating then the umpiring exams must be multi-choice and although I'm sure the exam papers told them otherwise they soon resorted to wild guessing.

Regardless, my effort in the first innings made me feel confident that I could compete. Yes, these guys were quick and they were accurate but I felt that if we fought hard we could succeed against them.

Twenty minutes into the second test and it was "wake up and smell the coffee Batchy" as they started bowling at incomprehensible speed. It was a harder deck than we'd had at Karachi but they were just lightning. It was my first experience of those two in full flight and Akram with his angles and his ability to swing it every which way was like nothing I'd ever faced before. It was difficult to be positive when I had so much uncertainty about where it was going and swaying out of the way of bouncers and having the ball follow you as if it had some sort of heat-seeking sensor was incredibly disconcerting. Akram would just come from nowhere, with no run-up, and sit you on your bum.

Phil Horne's discovery of the old ball after it had been

swapped soon made it clear that although these guys were good they were getting a little help from the three or four big strips that had been taken out of the ball. For Hogan to make a hundred against that sort of bowling was astonishing batting, all the more remarkable for the fact that he batted nine hours for 108 – a very un-Hoganlike rate.

Franko thought that the first hour was the easisest time to bat, which for cricketers is totally counter-intuitive. Taking the shine off the ball was the last thing we wanted to do and Franko (who batted for over an hour in all but one of his six test innings) said that the early bowling was quick but straight and after an hour just started to bend and slide everywhere.

We had a little practice in the nets with the artificially enhanced swing and, given the staggering results, were soon faced with the dilemma – do we stoop to their level or do we carry on stoically? Do we adopt the "when in Rome . . ." and "if you can't beat 'em . . ." mentality or do we try and take on them, their umpires and their dubious performance-enhancement methods. Urine samples are one thing but I didn't think we'd have to check their balls!

As a batsman struggling to succeed against the onslaught I was buggered if we were just going to let them run all over us. Looking back it may seem contrary to our own standards, but we had to compete and if local rules meant scratch hell out of the ball then deal me in. I actually got caught scratching away with a bottle top by an umpire, who had the cheek to say, "You can't do that – you are cheating."

"They're doing it, we're doing it," I replied. "Any problems?"

Not surprisingly, he didn't have an answer.

Phil Horne had come into the side and had the unenviable task of facing Younis the best part of a month after his last hit in the middle. Hornet hung in but first ball of one Younis over he got sweded and down he went. The remaining five balls were some of the fastest I've never seen, gold lettering and the smell of leather my most tangible memories. The game followed the normal course for the series with any player looking settled getting fired out and new batsmen struggling to get to grips with Younis. Akram was injured and didn't play, which was a big blessing but ultimately had no bearing on the result.

At the end of the tour I was mentally out of sorts in a way that I had never before experienced. I guess there was an element of fear, in that I didn't really know which way it was going, and at those speeds the margin of error is miniscule. The experience was bloody unpleasant and anyone who says they enjoyed it has an obscure sense of fun.

It was two and a half years before I had to fight my fear again and by now I'd made the transition to opening. I was going to be in a good position to test the validity of Franko's Pakistan assessment. In hindsight, I was never a proper test opener but with Jones, Crowe and Rutherford becoming established as a middle order combination it was my only real chance of securing a regular berth.

We were down to play the Pakis in Hamilton and like Perth several years earlier I had some great practice sessions before the test and felt positive about taking them on again. The ghosts of 1990 were still with me but the environment was better and I was a more experienced player. My confidence was about to be turned on its head.

We got the Pakis out for a couple of hundred and then had the happy hour at the end of the day where Younis and Akram could go flat out knowing they only had a few overs to bowl before stumps. The close fieldsmen took sledging to another level, making references to my mother among other things. I don't mind the normal gamesmanship of test cricket but these guys are way over the top. Survival was tricky, but Trustbank Park is a good seeing ground and I was picking it up OK when it was short. Stumps arrived with all wickets intact – runs were irrelevant, which was just as well because we hadn't exactly blasted it to all parts.

The next day was one of the most demanding I've ever experienced, even with the leg spinner Mushtaq bowling for much of the day. At the other end, Blair Hartland was gutsing it superbly, twice getting hit on the helmet. The second time, I wandered down to check on him and the side of his helmet had just caved in. There was blood running down the side of his face and I was sure he'd have to go off, but he just shook his head and got back into it which was an amazing display of courage. I'm sure he didn't pick up the second one that hit him and it takes a lot to carry on in those circumstances.

I got out just before stumps for 133 and to sit in the dressing room having made a hundred but still not feeling I had them mastered was a bewildering experience. It was as if I had survived from one ball to the next without really being "in"; something I had never felt at any level. Instead of feeling great and full of anticipation for the next innings it was as if I'd hardly made a run.

The bowlers performed superbly for the second time in the match and we were faced with what appeared a very gettable target with only Inzamam's seventy keeping them in the game. Well, it became clear that the Pakistani hatred of losing had not abated and it was like being back at Lahore in 1990. They threw everything at us and instead of seeing it like a basketball I was hopping all over the place. Early on in the piece Akram broke my finger and although I tried to conceal it they seemed to sense they'd done some damage.

There was something particularly predatory about them that evening – the close fielders like spectators watching a medieval joust, clapping and cheering as their victims were blasted out. The rest of the innings folded in the face of this fire and we were rumbled when victory was very achievable. My experience that evening had much to do with my problems with short stuff over subsequent seasons. I began to think about short pitched stuff to the point of obsession and my initial movement, which had been forward, was now back.

Lindsay Crocker, the former Northern Districts opener, came and saw me one day and kindly offered some help in dealing with the problem from a technical level. It had become obvious that my technique was suffering and he had some interesting observations about footwork and body position. I've worked hard with his suggestions and I believe they have contributed greatly to me recovering from a pretty shell-shocking experience.

At the end of the day I'm not totally suited to the test opener's role but if it means getting a chance to represent your country you take it. Looking back, I've had my best success down the order, but I was picked, I elected to play and I have to live with the results.

Fielding for long periods of time can take it out of you and my old friends the Pakistanis put me through my longest fielding ordeal. At Eden Park in 1989 they batted for seven or so sessions in amassing six hundred. I spent a lot of time in the covers and had to deal with Javed Miandad taunting us for 270 of those 600 runs. He would look at me as the bowler began to run in and motion with his head as to which way he was going to hit it. Sometimes he would bluff and sometimes he would hit it exactly where he had motioned! Those little games within games help to keep you alert and involved but it's draining to be on your feet and alert for all that time.

When I began opening for a few tests I began to understand why Wrighty used to get so toey when the last few opposition batsmen are in. To field for long periods and then have a ten minute break and go out and face the quicks as many times as Wrighty did is a very special achievement and speaks volumes for his mental toughness.

Physical fitness is often the key to overcoming mental tiredness but occasionally the tour arrangements leave you knackered. When we played Pakistan (them again) at Sialkot there was no suitable accommodation in the town so we had to leave where we were staying at 4.30 in the morning for a three-hour bus ride, arriving at 7.30 for a 9.00am start.

This is the red-eye with a difference and we were just getting settled in at the office when Younis started knocking our poles out left, right and centre. We finished the game, were driven home in the dark by a driver whose method of avoiding traffic was to veer onto the grass verge and arrived back at our hotel in the dead of night. What a super outing!

If you're on your game the crowd shouldn't be an issue but your first time in front of 50,000 at Melbourne can be pretty daunting. Richard Petrie came up after the fall of a wicket and said, "They're calling me names; what should I do?" – an interesting reaction for a guy who is generally not short of a word. It certainly demonstrates that too much attention to crowds and the wags within them can take your mind away from the things you should be focusing on. For most successful players, being in front of big crowds is a buzz and really lifts you.

Cricket, being a game of statistics and milestones, can change your mental state in the space of a run. You can be cruising along and dominating on 89, then a single will put you into the nineties, where you can become restricted and lose the freedom with which you have been playing. The field picks up and the game all of a sudden becomes hard again. Wrighty's charge down the wicket to Tuffnell at Christchurch when he was on 99 is a classic example of how the nineties can affect even the greats.

Another interesting ingredient in the mental side of the game is the way the mood in the dressing room can change, and how usually you are left on your own to deal with situations as they arise during a match. If things start to go wrong people tend to get very introverted and don't discuss their views on the events that are unfolding.

I've always felt there is much to be gained from talking about what is going on and developing ideas and strategies for the time which complement the overall game plan. It would certainly be a far more positive way of contributing to the team than moping around the dressing room.

Preparing mentally for cricket can take a number of forms. At the end of the day it's not which method you choose but that you do it at all, and of course a method that you are comfortable with and which brings you results.

During the Ashes tour to England in 1989 I spent a lot of time watching the Aussie bowlers, taking notes about what little quirks they might exhibit and the variety of deliveries they might bowl. It was invaluable preparation when it came to facing them in Perth.

When I went to India for the first time in 1988 I had a tough time facing the spinners and, not surprisingly, dealing with bat-pad decisions from Indian umpires. I knew I had to find a method to combat them and spent hours facing youngsters in the nets honing a technique. It was my first tour away, the coach of the time was of little value in batting technique and I knew I had to deal with this on my own, or the tour was going to be a disaster.

On the surface this appears to fit more into the realm of technical preparation, but what it did was allow me to take the field feeling positive about my chances of success. To go from "Well, they're just going to fire me anyway" to "If I play this way I will succeed against these guys" is a huge mental turnaround and one I'm sure allowed me to make a far greater contribution with the bat in the two remaining tests.

Routines are also crucial in getting the mind right. Often this is day-by-day routines during a test match, but frequently it is about what you did the last time you played at a certain ground or against a certain team. If you were successful at a particular ground and had a run around the arena before the start of play there is something comforting about repeating the procedure before the next time you play.

There is, at times, a fine line between mental preparation and superstition, but it is all about doing everything you need to do to take the field feeling positive and that there are no extraneous reasons why you shouldn't succeed.

Superstitions do abound in cricket, though, from the

famous numbers 87 and 111 and people putting a particular pad on first every time. Their existence was brought home to me when I turned up to a game in my training gear and put my after-match clobber on the wall hook. Jeff Crowe recoiled like a vampire in the face of a crucifix when he saw the belt I had chosen had ducks all the way around it – he actually banished it from the dressing room. I thought it was quite a fashionable item and hadn't seen its darker side.

I enjoy the mental side of the game and the challenges it imposes on you. There is a high degree of mental strength required to succeed at the top level and I've had some big obstacles to overcome. The Pakistanis have been my greatest mental challenge and I would dearly love to finish my career with that demon well and truly exorcised.

They Love Me Not

When you've been out of nick and the phone rings you can put money on the fact that the caller is not the bearer of great news. "Oh Mark, we just wanted to let you know you won't be involved . . . We've decided to bring in . . . But the door's not shut . . ." All the cliches are trotted out but really you can't wait to put down the phone. There's a churning in the pit of your stomach and the self-doubt hits in. Is this the end? Am I just not good enough any more? Surely they can't think he's better than me?

You think about running the bath of self pity and having a good old wallow but what good would that do – then you think a beer might be the answer, and you know you've hit rock bottom when you start feeling better because "at least you've got your health".

Unless you're a Crowe or a Hadlee it's a feeling every cricketer is going to experience from time to time.

For me, the only pleasant memory of being dropped has been to go and join the Central Districts boys and get my game back together. They have always helped me put things in perspective, they've given me confidence, and most importantly they've helped me get back in the national side.

The first time I was left out of the test team was against Sri Lanka in 1991. I missed out in the first innings (along with everyone else) and sat in the stand with the pads on for ten hours in the second innings before having an hour at the crease for a not out. I was left out for the next match, which I found bewildering given that I was averaging in the forties in tests and Rutherford, who also missed out but was retained, sported an average in the teens. Nevertheless, it did make me wake up and I knew that I didn't have the runs to justify inclusion as of right.

I experienced similar emotions in 1992 but I knew then I was struggling and the fact that we were beaten always means people will be replaced. In many ways that selection did me good because I was able to get away and work at my game and start putting together a few scores. Had I been retained I am sure I would have continued to struggle.

The tour of England saw me on the scrap heap again and I have dealt with that tour elsewhere in the book.

At the end of 1995 I got the dreaded call soon after the rain-affected tour of India. I'd had a bit of trouble against Srinath on the dewy wickets (we started at 9.00am) but generally felt my game was in reasonable shape. I'd made two hundreds and my final test innings of the tour had brought a fifty so I didn't feel as if I was dreadfully out of nick – the caller thought otherwise.

It was certainly good of Glenn Turner to give me a call and as usual he was honest in his assessment of where I stood. He cited lack of form and told me just to get out and score some runs, but I had only an average start in the Cup and he felt I wasn't getting my runs quickly enough. In my last Cup match I scored 90 in as many balls and proceeded to have my best season ever, scoring heavily throughout the year.

Unfortunately, Glenn had formulated his side without me in it, and I was notified of my non-selection in the midst of scoring 200 against Northern. When Mark Bailey joined the team in the West Indies it was clear I was far from uppermost in the coach's mind.

Amidst all the runs of last season I began to be flooded by questions suggesting a personality clash between myself and Turner. I had been supportive of Turner and had no problems with the disciplines he was introducing to the side. I think any personality clash theories demonstrate a lack of appreciation of Turner, who is far too clinical an individual to be side-tracked by that sort of thing. I use the word clinical in the sense that had I scored heavily in India I have no doubt he would have picked me even if I was his least favourite person on the planet.

My disappointment at missing out was exacerbated by the fact that World Cups are special and there was every chance that my last opportunity to compete had passed me by.

I guess any disappointment with Turner comes down to his inability to apply his own philosophies when he himself was dumped. Instead of taking his dumping with good grace he chose to pillory New Zealand Cricket and make mystical remarks such as "all will be revealed in time".

Like the players under him, Turner must stand or fall on his record, particularly as he put little store in the softer measures like ability to manage people. Frankly, that record is only average and although I applaud many of the initiatives he put in place I saw no reason for him to play on a small measure of public opinion by making derogatory remarks about Chris Doig and his administration.

New Zealand Cricket remained silent throughout, leaving Turner's comments to reek of the bitterness he claimed not to possess. When he dropped me, Turner said to go out and get some runs. It's a shame he didn't stay out of the media and heed his own advice.

It is also hard to be on the other side of the selection fence. After an heroic Greg Loveridge innings against Wellington at the end of 1995, the Central Districts boys were in great heart and after a slow start felt they had turned the corner. The selectors felt otherwise and five guys learnt that they woudn't be required for the next game. It was a sobering experience to see the desolation on the faces of guys who would do anything to don the CD colours.

Communication when you're dropped has not always been that special. For Turner to make the effort was great and I appreciated hearing it from him rather than through the media, which has happened. The treatment of Ken Rutherford when he was stripped of the captaincy and left out of the side was pretty ordinary and, communication breakdown or not, that should never have been allowed to happen.

It has not only been when leaving players out that the administration have performed poorly. Many times we have signed tour contracts in airport lounges on the way to the destination, which is unsatisfactory given that many players have managers who should be aware of what the contract entails. The contract we were asked to sign before the Indian tour in 1995 stipulated a number of things, notably about promotional activity and the writing of biographies. Lee Germon did his best to get us to sign but at the end of the day he shouldn't have to be involved in cajoling players into signing contracts.

The contract for each tour should be agreed well before departure day so that everyone gets on the plane in complete understanding of the respective obligations of the players and the management. It doesn't seem too much to ask to have the contract as an integral part of the tour preparation.

Consistency is the key with all of these things – if there is a clear procedure for communication with players who are left out, for tour preparation and indeed for selection, then the incidence of misunderstandings and things "falling through the cracks" will be greatly reduced. Michael Owens was unaware that he was on standby for the tour to England in 1994 and subsequently was well short of a gallop when he joined the team. By working hard at his fitness he soon came up to speed, but it was unfair on him that he should be so ill-informed.

Too many players have been victims of inconsistent selection policies – one minute good enough to be in the XI, the next not good enough to be in a squad of 14. Willie Watson, a guy who put in some superb performances for his country, must have wondered where he was at times and there are a number of others who were probably entitled to some answers. Again, clarity is important in that each player should be aware of what specifically is required and the time frame allowed for the achievement of those goals.

Although I'm in favour of a detailed process for leaving a player out in terms of accurate communication, I also believe the onus is on the player to think hard about why he's not there. Was my preparation up to its usual standard? What sort of errors did I make on the day? Who can help me with my game? It is hard work and performance that guarantee us our spots. Seeking answers from outsiders may get you some interesting replies, but are the right questions being asked?

There is really no substitute for working hard at your game – seeking opportunities to have a net or a bat in the middle. For everyone, from test player down, the opportunity to just get out and have a bat is one that should never be forsaken. It is important too that players back themselves, even in the face of an understandable loss of self-esteem. A run of outs doesn't make you a bad player, but if you are not prepared to front up and work hard to get your game back in order the self-doubt will remain and the chances of reaching your potential will be limited.

Tour From Hell

I've always enjoyed touring with the New Zealand cricket team. The opportunity to compete on famous grounds against the best players in the world and to experience other countries and their lifestyles at the same time has been a genuine highlight of my career. My enjoyment has only been coloured on a couple of tours, the common denominator on both occasions being one G.P. Howarth. I had a little bit to do with Howarth over the years and respected him for his fine record as a player and captain but his inability to organise himself, let alone an international sports team, has in my experience been woeful.

It would be wrong to lay all my troubles of 1994 at Geoff Howarth's door but when it is clear the coach doesn't want you in the side it makes breaking into it somewhat difficult! The environment generated by Howarth was totally foreign to what I considered appropriate for a New Zealand team and I'm sure my attitude was influenced accordingly.

After a festival match against some of the game's greats, the summer of 1993/94 began in Western Australia where the big quickie Jo Angel broke the same finger that Wasim

Akram had rearranged in Hamilton. We lost that match, against the state side, by an innings and I was out for three weeks, which unfortunately coincided with the first test in Perth.

Early in the tour, Howarth treated us to some of his legendary antics and at a team dinner was soon gassed and obnoxious. At one stage he lifted a wine bottle to his eye and peered in at close range searching desperately for more. The fact that all this was in front of the team was deplorable and a clear exhibition of the guy's standards. I enjoy a few quiets with the best of them but to see a guy in his position destroy any respect the team may have had for him was alarming so early into his tenure.

The tour was not a good one with only Rutherford and Blain showing any sort of consistency among the batsmen. I started at opener but dropped down the list after the first two tests, never really getting going in any of the matches. We were not helped by a pretty brittle bowling attack, worsened by the withdrawal of Cairns before the Hobart test. The Australians were playing well, with Warne mystifying most of us and their batsmen using the series to improve already impressive records.

I was named vice-captain when Rutherford took over and considered I gave him pretty good support – he became a bit of a loner and certainly felt the pressure of leading an outclassed New Zealand side.

We went straight into a Benson & Hedges series against Australia and South Africa and after picking up some good wins and looking like we would qualify we blew it against South Africa in Perth and missed the finals.

Unfortunately, the summer was not going to get any easier as the green men of Pakistan arrived in early 1994. They were almost becoming the default option and played in New Zealand for four summers in a row from 1992 – great for the public to see the two Ws in action, but not exactly the batsmen's first request in terms of a test match opponent. In 1994, with most batsmen struggling for form and our best player on the physio's bench, they were among the last people we needed to see.

Captaining a Board XI, I experienced at first hand Salim Malik's chicanery when it came coin-toss time. As the home captain, I tossed and Malik called heads. When the coin landed on tails I immediately said, "We'll bat."

"No, Mark," Malik replied, "we will bat."

I was amazed. "Salim, you called heads."

"No, I called tails."

I wasn't wearing this. "We are batting; good luck with the game," I said, and walked away.

That he repeated the stunt in the test match only a week or so later showed he would have a crack anywhere. Such behaviour certainly adds credence to the Australian bribery allegations.

The first test was played on a deck that looked remarkably similar to one I had prepared out in West Auckland as a kid. It was a real make sure your premiums are up to date job and fifteen wickets fell on the first day. I had managed to get into Mushtaq a bit but eventually got out to him just when Jonesy and I were getting a reasonable stand organised. Amazingly, we managed a first innings lead but didn't enjoy it for long and were skittled for a little over a hundred, which they knocked off five down. For a test match to be over just after lunch on the third day, and have 35 wickets fall, says enough about the quality of the track.

Although Blainy and Danny got their highest test scores, we took a good old-fashioned towelling in Wellington and there was little to be encouraged by as we approached the final test.

I had made two forties so wasn't totally distraught about my form but I was well done in Christchurch. They got the reverse swing going well and I was struggling to the extent that when I was put out of my misery I had batted forty minutes for one – I just couldn't lay wood on it and even a couple of World Cup whooshes couldn't get it off the square. Thankfully, Youngy and Thommo played out of their skins to snatch a victory. Thommo did what only Glenn Turner, Jeremy Coney and John Wright had done in scoring an unbeaten hundred to win a test match. It was a superb knock and to get a hundred against those guys off only 140-odd balls has to rate as one of the great innings in our test history.

As we faced India, I was struggling and getting back into bad habits against the short ball. Srinath soon had me tidied up, aiming a string of deliveries into my ribs before feeding me a wide one which I nicked. In the second innings the cricketing gods reminded me I was still far from their good books when I hit Kumble hard to mid wicket only to have Manjrekar pull in a blinder at short leg. I was in the twenties and feeling good which made it all the more frustrating. The only really bright spot in the match from a New Zealand point of view was an elegant 92 by which Stephen Fleming signalled his arrival in international cricket.

With the tour of England looming, I started to feel my poor run of form would count against me and there was a real chance I would not be selected. There were a number of strong candidates for batting spots and the advent of Fleming and the return of Crowe, both certainties, made my chances rather slim. I'd played a few tests without scoring fifty and although I hadn't resigned myself to missing out I was certainly preparing for the worst.

When the side was named with me in it I was one very relieved cricketer. I don't recall anyone else making a swag of runs and demanding inclusion but England is often used to blood players because of the large number of first class games and that could well have sealed my fate. Looking at the other batsmen – Young, Hartland, Pocock, Fleming, Crowe, Rutherford and Thomson – I knew I would have to score heavily to be in the team for the major matches.

Shortly before the team left for England I was due to marry Marina Whiteman. As is the custom, I had a bit of a stag do and halfway through the night, while walking to the bar, my knee just gave way underneath me. Down I went, like a sack of spuds. Although the source of great hilarity to my mates, who saw it as representative of inebriation rather than any structural problems with the knee, I knew that a trip to Barry Tietjens was on the cards. Barry had worked his magic with me before and soon had me patched up and functional again.

On April 9, at St Mary's Church, Marina and I were married in front of our family and friends. It was a special day and we celebrated with a superb breakfast in the Auckland Grammar School hall. Wedded bliss could be enjoyed for only a week or so before I was off to London to join the team, who had been involved in an Austral-Asian competition in Sharjah.

At the first team meeting in London we were going through the normal administrative details which all touring sides sort out. Things like laundry, autographs, entertainment (which seemed to be a priority for the coach) and tickets were all discussed and the appropriate committees formed.

Toward the end of the meeting Mike Sandlant made a statement about wives on tour which, with Marina virtually in the air and the tickets booked and paid for, I was horrified to hear. Some of the players had heard of impending policy at the Shell awards dinner, held shortly before the team's departure, but as a non-attender of that function I had no idea that any such policy was being formulated and certainly wasn't aware it was now in place.

Apparently, it had been agreed that no wives would be allowed on tour until June 16, which coincided with the second test at Lord's. It was the first I had heard about it and asked to meet separately to find a solution. I met with Crowe, Rutherford, Howarth and Sandlant and was informed that Marina would not be permitted to join the team. I found it hard to take, particularly when Mike's wife was on tour and Geoff's partner was going to be around.

Had the policy been clearly spelt out prior to the tour we could easily have made the appropriate arrangements.

Nothing had been said, though, and this was way past the time to be discussing it. In the end we worked out a solution and I was grateful to Mike, who faxed New Zealand Cricket and smoothed the way. Rutherford was anti the whole deal and continued to display his feelings to Marina after she arrived, which was pretty distasteful.

Much has been made of my travelling to grounds alone on that tour. On every tour of England, Air New Zealand supply a luxury coach and two cars to get the team around. The cars are useful in case of emergency and every now and then players will jump in and try to get to the next destination a bit quicker, rather than spend a long time on the coach. It gives a little bit of flexibility and allows guys the chance to stop for a pub lunch or pick up some incidentals that aren't on the coach route. Early in the tour, guys are pretty keen on the cars but as they get a little more jaded toward the end it is very difficult to find drivers.

It was only a week or so into the tour when we discovered that Alice Elizabeth Greatbatch was on the way. Unfortunately, Marina had awful morning sickness and spent much of the tour exploring the toilet bowls of England. With Marina being sick it made sense for me to drive a car when we could and other players enjoyed the freedom when the opportunity arose. To assert I was driving a car because I had tossed the toys out of the cot is nonsense and I was as happy as anyone to join the team on the bus. The fact of the matter was that the cars had to get to the grounds and there weren't too many queuing up to do it by the end of the tour.

Geoff Howarth was an unfortunate influence on the tour and if it weren't for Mike Sandlant being such a nice guy I believe he would never have taken the team to South Africa. I hated the way he was running things and it burned me up to see such a seat of the pants style in charge of the team. After the first meeting in London we didn't get together as a team until the first one-dayer; this on a tour with a number of young guys who would have thrived on some sensible discussion on how their games were going, what lessons could be learned from the games we had played and what goals we should have for games to follow.

Practices were excessive and endless nets are a sure sign that the coach has run out of ideas. We would train for three and a half hours the day before games; way over the top, particularly in a side beset by injuries. The training sessions were in stark contrast to the short, sharp and superbly organised sessions we had enjoyed during the 1992 World Cup, when training was over in a couple of hours and everyone felt sharp when it came to match day.

Howarth had a few things to say to me in the nets but was far keener on discussing technique in the bar. I had no interest in this sort of approach and was completely unreceptive. I don't mind talking cricket over a beer but specifics on technique should not be discussed over a few lagers. This is not my hobby, it's my job, and it should be afforded the appropriate environment and time.

There are enough stories about Howarth's drinking antics and they need no elaboration. Suffice to say he was a very grumpy man in the morning and had an unusual habit of wearing his sunglasses to breakfast!

From a playing point of view, I had what can only be described as an average tour. I finished with an average in the mid-thirties, which is really the bare minimum for an international batsman and far from where I wanted to be. I started the tour off OK but was getting mainly thirties and forties, never really being able to kick on for a big score. With Crowe, Rutherford and Fleming pretty much set I had to compete against Thommo (who had his off-spinners to throw into the equation) or have another crack at grabbing an opener's berth.

My double failure at Middlesex effectively removed me from international contention and it wasn't until the true extent of Blair Pocock's injury was discovered that a hole appeared at the top of the order. Pokey had thrown his shoulder out in the match before the second test and although selected he was never really fit enough to play and struggled for the remainder of the tour.

I made 80 against Derby and was back in the side at Old Trafford, once again at the top of the order. Here I was back opening with a head full of troubles and facing the slippery Gough in his first test. I got him away to a good start by nicking one to Hick and then managed to break my thumb in the field. My lack of form and knackered thumb conspired for me to produce one of my least memorable test knocks as I spent two hours in the second innings poking and prodding, barely able to hold the bat. I felt like a cricketing imbecile.

The end of the tour was a blessing for me and I was pleased to finally leave such a shambolic environment. Hard as it is to believe, it was an environment that was going to get worse.

By now the drums were beating and it was clear that a number of people were unhappy with Howarth and his methods. Rod Fulton, who was then the director of cricket, polled the players on their satisfaction with Geoff Howarth. An astonishing 75 percent of the team said they did not like the way he was running things, but at a national training camp later that year Fulton called us in and asked for our opinion of Howarth.

I was sure we had been loud and clear in the questionnaire and although it had been anonymous I had no qualms about signing it – I was not comfortable with hiding behind anonymity, particularly when I was being critical. It was as if Fulton was asking "but what do you *really* think?" as if we might suddenly change our minds.

Blair Hartland said that he didn't feel his lack of form on tour could be put solely to Howarth and I think we all agreed with that, but his disorganisation and extra-curricular antics were well beyond a joke. For reasons known only to a few, he was retained and the charade was maintained until it was blown apart in South Africa.

It is a shame that what may well be my last tour of

England should be such a forgettable one. England holds a special place in my cricketing life and only 1994 blights what has been a place of achievement and great enjoyment over many years. I didn't score heavily enough early in the tour to make the test side and I can live with that but to see someone in charge of the New Zealand side behave with such disregard for the position was hard to take. At a time when the team and the captain needed direction and advice, the coach was found lacking – or, more to the point, he was found in a wine bar.

A Square Turner

In the middle of 1995 the squad got together with Glenn Turner, who had been re-appointed as coach after the Geoff Howarth debacle. It was my first cricketing involvement with Turner since the pre-World Cup campaign in 1987. I have always been impressed with Turner's knowledge of cricket and his technical proficiency. There are few in the country and probably not many in the world who can match his tactical appreciation and strategic view.

Going into the camp I was very positive about his appointment and although I thought Rutherford still merited a role as a player I was also pleased about the change in the captaincy. I was well aware going into the season that Turner was not likely to pat me on the back every day, and it was well recognised that "warm fuzzies" just aren't his thing. That said, when he did say "well done" you knew you'd done bloody well. We needed discipline and direction and Glenn Turner was the ideal individual to provide it.

The camp dealt with a number of things and Turner outlined his philosophies on everything from team discipline to dealing with sponsors. He invited comment, but I think had it pretty clear in his own mind how it was going to be, regardless of our input. Loyalty to the team was paramount and I admired him for making it so prominent in his blueprint.

We went to Darwin to prepare for what was to be a very long programme and immediately were struck by the different level of organisation and discipline. Everything we did was purposeful, and we measured our performances at matches and at training. If we had 30 high catches, we recorded it, if we did 10 minutes of sprinting in our batting gear, we recorded it, so by tour end we had an accurate dossier on all the work we had put in and what our thoughts were on the innings we played.

We worked very hard and by the end of the tour everyone had put in a good performance or two. Geoff Allot of Canterbury had a top little tour and ended up grabbing a test spot by season end.

I roomed with Hogan and early in the tour Turner would come in to our room and ask us out for a meal or just for a chat. I enjoyed talking with him about the game but I noticed early on that he had very firm views on the game, almost to the point of inflexibility. If Hogan or I offered a different view his response was always "yes but" rather than "good point". Maybe I just didn't make any.

The beauty of Darwin, apart from getting the team together, was playing against top opposition (Victoria featured Warne and Jones). Too often we had fronted up on tours with minimal cricket and it was a pleasant change to arrive "cricket fit".

We acclimatised further with a week in Bombay, which was another bonus, and then headed back to Rajkot for the tour opener. Danny Morrison was the only other "survivor" from 1988 and we were undismayed to discover that the Hotel Jayson had not changed hands or been refurbished, but had in fact been demolished. The hotel was gone but the impeccable service remained and we were looking forward to a bat on the flattest thing since Cher before implants.

I had been working hard with Turner on a technique against the spinners designed to "flat bat" square rather than punch straight. With the slower wickets the ball would often not arrive, so waiting and hitting through and around point seemed a better option. I managed to get a ton in my first innings of the tour, facing a rejuvenated Hirwani for much of the time. All the batsmen got runs in one of the innings and it was an excellent way to kick the tour off. Azza got a hundred for them and wandered past one on purpose, although Has will claim he did him in the air.

The bat he was using, which must have looked pretty large to the bowlers, was emblazoned with Reebok stickers, an arrangement that was rumoured to be bringing him $US150,000. It certainly brought home the commercial advantages of being a big star in a country of hundreds of millions of people.

Ranji Trophy holders Bombay were our next opponent and boasted in their ranks the likes of Tendulkar, Manjrekar and Kambli. We struggled a bit after a late start with the ball dipping around a bit in the steambath conditions. Mhambrey slipped one into my helmet, a nice little wake up call. I got to 89 by stumps and probably dropped a couple of kg in the process. I managed to pick up the next 11 in the morning and promptly got out, which the coach didn't consider too clever. I think he was happy with my performance but was keen to make sure I kept thinking about the next innings which is obviously the right way to go.

Our fitness was in no doubt as Plums had brought an exercise bike on tour and would set it up each morning in the dressing room. It was an excellent way to warm up or down, or just for a straight-out fitness session. The bike had an odometer on it and it wasn't long before time for distance records were being bandied about. I was the holder for a while which didn't sit well with Adam Parore and he was determined to unseat me. Sadly, the only thing unseated was him as the bike collapsed under the strain of his furious pedalling.

We had a couple of meetings before the first test and although we were well prepared we seemed a bit tense, which is the wrong sort of nervousness to take into a test. I'd been positive in my two hundreds and wanted to take that approach into the game, but we lost wickets early, including my own. Were it not for a superb knock from Lee, who played the spinners magnificently, we would have been disgraced rather than merely embarrassed. It was all the more impressive given that it was his first test.

The ball was moving around a bit and Cairns, Nash and Morrison exploited the conditions well restricting them to a lead of 80. Cairnsy bowled a couple of superb spells and really troubled Azza who had top-scored with 87.

A lead of 80 should not have been insurmountable but we were soon in trouble again at the top of the order. Youngy got caught on the crease and was LB to Prabhakar and the same bowler knocked my poles over with a relatively straight one – nice test match Batchy. I'm sure he biffs the odd one and this one just seemed to get to me before I thought it would. Whatever the reason, it started a procession and it was only Flem and Lee who showed any sort of form, with Lee again top-scoring.

Needing only 150, Jadeja boofed it and Prabhakar blocked it, between them ensuring a comfortable win. Harty bowled well for us but we were a very disappointed side in the way we had performed. There were a lot of teens and a few twenties in the scorebook and we just weren't kicking on from reasonable starts. The seamers were in good form and with reasonable totals to bowl at would make us a competitive unit.

Unfortunately, Madras was just mud. It rained and rained and we ended up out of our heads in frustration. We had to put up with lots of Prabhakar and only Tendulkar played an innings of anything like test quality. For an entire match to produce 144 runs and two wickets demonstrates the desperate weather conditions we were faced with. The approaches to the ground just stank and one morning our bus became stuck in the mud and had to be dragged out by the police.

We did manage an open wicket session after the match was called off and I got a good insight into the competitive edge of Dion Nash. I'd been batting for a wee while and he came in and bounced me. Next ball he did the same so I whistled it, suggesting he might want to put a few men back if he was going to bowl like that. He was adamant it was out and it got pretty heated, which I think was indicative of the frustration we were all feeling.

The Colts game between the tests was unremarkable other than the fact that we did get on the field and for the quality of the bats they were using. They were tiny little guys but they hit a couple over the ropes that were 12s. They were huge hits and although timing has much to do with it I'm sure their sticks had a big bearing as well.

It was good to get some cricket in at last and we were looking forward to Cuttack, but down came the rain again and that was just about that. There was a chance that we might have played at Eden Gardens in Calcutta but they were still putting the finishing touches on it for the forthcoming World Cup.

So it was off to Cuttack and on the way to the ground we passed a river where no fewer than forty people were having a morning constitutional in the river. It was a real all-purpose piece of water with laundry, teeth cleaning and the aforementioned all part of the deal.

Cairns and Nash bowled well again and we bowled them out for three hundred. It was a non-event test, unfortunately, and we wandered out to start our first innings on the morning of day five. It would rain every morning and consequently the ground just never quite dried out. Twosey was having his first bat on his tenth day of test cricket!

Srinath was as demanding as ever but we managed to put on 86 for the first wicket before Twosey was out. I got 50 before padding one in close and getting sawn off. It was incredibly frustrating, particularly when it was my last opportunity to compile a decent score in the tests.

In every respect it was a disaster of a series and questions must be asked about the wisdom of granting matches to those venues during the monsoon season. I am sure it will not happen again but that is little consolation to the players from both sides who loitered around the stadiums for days on end.

We were delayed leaving a Cuttack because of a riot in one of the villages we were supposed to pass through. We ended up taking cabs on a slightly more circuitous route, but did catch sight of some of the carnage and it looked pretty serious.

The Tata Steel company were effectively our hosts for the first one-dayer. They are huge employers in the city of Jamshedpur and own the ground that we played on. The CEO of Tata invited the team to his mansion for a function, which was a lovely occasion, and in a nice gesture we were all presented with a pair of steel bails. I was getting my poles knocked over a bit so I thought of taking them out to the middle.

All the one-dayers were played on small grounds so 250 was a minimum for the side batting first. The games started at nine in the morning and followed a similar pattern. The side winning the toss would insert and on all but one occasion knocked off the total. The reasons for this were twofold; it was difficult to bat first thing in the morning when there was a bit of juice in the track, and it was easier to chase on the small grounds where boundaries were not difficult to collect.

In the first match we were chasing 230-odd and Hogan and Flem played superbly. Flem in particular was in great touch and helped Hogan through an uncharacteristically slow start. It was a start that did not elude the coach, who commented, "The first forty were pretty embarrassing but you've probably done enough to get picked for the next one." Nothing if not honest!

Visual Impact /Richard Hare

Big celebrations for every World Cup wicket – this one is Hanse Cronje's leaving do.

Greatbatch Collection

Boonie goes undercover at the Adelaide Oval.

It's never too serious with 'Chilla' Blain.

Greatbatch Collection

Over page: Boofing Aaqib into the stand – 1992 World Cup semi-final v Pakistan.

Where would we have been without them in '92 – Plums and Wal.

I'VE MANAGED TO CUT THE BOUNDARIES DOWN TO SIZE..

SLASH

GREATBATCH

ELLISON

Ellison is impressed.

ANZ Bank
ANZ Bank
MATATA
RUGBY
SELECTOR
SPORTS FOUNDAT

IMRAN
KHANT
ONE WORLD OF SPORT

I wasn't the only Kiwi giving them grief in '89.

I guess they've got to draw it as they see it.

Greatbatch Collection

Get up early and you'll catch the big ones – Yeah, right!

Gotcha!

The Indians squared up in game two with only Nathe getting away on a patchy, difficult track – 140 was a walk in the park and we never even got the crowd interested. The consistency that we were striving for was proving elusive and we wanted to get it right in the next one.

Nathe and I cocked it up a bit, unfortunately, and Srinath bowled a lively pace which was tricky to get away. We used up too many balls and only Cairnsy playing out of his skin for 103 gave us anything to bowl at. It really was one of the great one-day knocks and deserved to be a match winner. Manjrekar, Azza and Kambli matched him blow for blow and they got them with five overs to spare – those guys sure know how to smash a cricket ball.

We were now facing a must-win if the series was to stay alive. At the team meeting the night before the game, Turner and Lee led the discussion as had been the procedure throughout the tour. After a while I piped up and sought clarification on the opener's role, largely because I'd made a hash of it in the previous match. Before too long others joined in the conversation and the meeting began to flourish as ideas and thoughts were exchanged. At one end of the room it was clear Turner was uncomfortable with the way the meeting had developed, which was puzzling considering everyone was so positive.

The next day we went out and boofed it everywhere with Nathe making a great hundred. Hogan and Flem contributed sixties and we ended up making 348, a huge score even on a small ground. There were a lot of red missiles flying around when the Indians batted and I was delighted to dive and stop a Tendulkar drive which he thought had beaten me – he had no chance of getting back and their key man was gone. Remarkably, they were eventually dismissed for 249, remarkable because they got there in 39.3 overs! Although a great display of hitting, it wasn't enough against such a huge total.

Our delight at levelling the series was tempered when we learned that several of the crowd had been killed during the match. A section of one of the stands had collapsed and several people were crushed, which was extraordinarily sad. Apparently a meeting was held at the lunch break debating whether the match should continue, but it was decided that there was danger of more loss of life through riots if the game was called off.

The next night we were invited to a barbecue (more trouble than they're worth in recent seasons) by the TWI team, the television company covering the tour. On a very pleasant occasion it was nice to enjoy a beer with Stockley and Ravi Shastri, who were calling the matches. I left with a couple of the TV guys who were heading back to the hotel and the team bus left about twenty minutes later. A few guys kicked on and put in a late one, risky behaviour with an 8.30 training the next day.

Twosey and I were rooming together and popped down for breakfast in good shape. Just as we were pouring a bit of hot milk on the Kornies, Lee and Turner came over, sat down with us and started asking a few questions about the previous night. "What time did Crowey get home?" We both gave it the wise monkey. They began to write down two lists of players – the early guys and the late guys.

"A few of the guys," Turner said ominously, "had late nights last night."

I suggested we have a bit of a sweat to start training just to blow it out of all of us, but Turner said, "No, I'm going to teach these guys a lesson."

The bus left for training with a full complement although one of our number was in awful nick and seemed to be having some trouble putting one leg in front of the other. We got to the ground and an announcement was made. A list of names was read out – "these players will have nets this morning." A second list was read out – "these players will have a fitness session this morning and will return for nets this afternoon." The groans were audible and some players were livid, having been wrongly put in the "Bad Boys Club".

The fact that it was on the eve of the final one-dayer meant the guys were going to spend an inordinate amount of time training.

Early in the fitness session Cairnsy just bailed, claiming to have pulled a hamstring. I had my bat, then changed. Cairnsy was nowhere to be seen. It turned out he had taken a cab and headed back to the hotel.

Although Cairnsy fronted for the afternoon session he took no part in training and appeared to be sticking to the hamstring tale for all he was worth. At the team meeting Turner announced that Crowe was out with injury and Adam would play and that "Chris Cairns will be replaced by Simon Doull".

What followed was an interesting exercise in psychology which didn't work for me, that's for sure. "New Zealand sides after winning well often don't play well in their next match, and New Zealand sides don't play well when they're about to go home from a tour," Turner pronounced, adding, "I just hope we don't lose by too much tomorrow." The guys were stunned.

Unfortunately, Turner's words at the team meeting were more prophetic than motivational and we crashed in the worst possible way. Srinath and Kumble bowled superbly and we went belly up in a big hurry. It was a sad end to what had been a hell of a series and we picked the biggest game for our worst performance.

Cairnsy was in charge of autographs on tour and came up to me too soon after I was dismissed. "Sign these," he demanded.

"I'll do them when I'm ready," I replied.

"What do you mean?" he challenged.

By now I'd had enough. "Get out of my sight." I was livid and still can't understand what he was trying to achieve by his non-playing stance.

The postscript to the story is the most disappointing part of a pretty sad tale. The next time a New Zealand side was picked Cairns was in it with only a fine for his actions.

There is no doubt he is a rare talent and puts bums on seats but you cannot put yourself in front of your teammates when it comes to representing your country. The treatment meted out was way too lenient and the West Indian fiasco demonstrated that no lesson had been learnt. I hope his prodigious ability will be matched by loyalty to his team and maybe his inability to secure a contract may make him take a broader view of the responsibilities inherent in being part of a team.

The management style of Turner and Alabaster is not for everyone and Cairnsy was far from on his own in having problems with them. The disciplines and organisation were fine to begin with but later became pernickety and ultimately trivial. In the Colts game in India, Adam came into the dressing room after making 96 and threw his bat hard into his gear. Nothing was said at the time and it wasn't until a team meeting before the third test that it was announced his actions would earn him a severe reprimand.

We were dumbfounded – it had happened in the dressing room, no-one was affected and compared to some of the famous bat throwers of the past was a pretty tame expression of frustration. When I proffered these thoughts, supported by Thommo and Hogan, Turner got angry. "You guys made the rules [referring to the mid-winter camp]," he said, "and anyone who doesn't stick to them is out." Debate over sentencing or the hint of an appeal was not even close to getting on the agenda.

It was becoming increasingly difficult to find a beer in the dressing room, and while I completely understood the re-hydration policy, a couple of lagers after a win is hardly going to render anyone a health risk. I struggled a bit with Alabaster and will talk more on him in the administrators section. I believe in rules, but not pedantry, and I believe at times they crossed the line, claiming to treat us as adults yet not including flexibility in their management philosophy.

Friends, Kiwis, Countrymen

Every player's career is really just a sub-set of a much greater whole. Some players enjoy greater chunks of the limelight, some players detest greater chunks of the limelight and some players are just happy to be there, competing for their country. I've had my moments in the sun, but I've also had my dark days and those are the days when teammates and friends assume even greater importance. It is a pleasure to be able to acknowledge the special players with whom I've competed and share my thoughts on how they have enriched the experience of playing for New Zealand.

It will come as no surprise that Martin Crowe is first on the list. The players to follow are in no particular order but Hogan is a guy with whom my cricket started and he undoubtedly has been the biggest influence on my career. At his best he is on a totally different plane from the rest of us; at his worst he is just better. Watching him play was inspirational, in that he gave you the benchmark for which to strive. At a First XI cricket barbecue in 1979 I remember saying "I just want to be half as good as Hogan" when asked about my aspirations. I got a bit of razzing for it, but I believed that if I could achieve it I wouldn't be a bad player. The technique I use for switching on and off comes from Hogan and there are numerous times he has helped with the technical side of my game.

We didn't bat together in tests that often but it was great batting with him in Perth in 1989, when in the first innings we went after them and put on a pretty brisk sort of partnership.

Two Crowe innings stand out – his ton at Manchester in 1994 was pure control and fluency and he was in another league as the rest of us scratched about. The other occasion was against the West Indies when they started to sniff a chance in the World Cup match at Auckland in 1992. We'd lost a couple of wickets and they seemed to bowl faster and faster as the afternoon wore on. Unfortunately for them, Hogan just kept hitting straighter and straighter, bashing the ball back past them. In a tournament of great knocks I think this was the greatest.

Tactically he was outstanding and the success in the World Cup was as much to do with the way he handled the bowlers and the field placings as any individual performances with bat or ball.

Having a good friend in the dressing room has been fantastic – the good times are even better and the defeats are easier to bear. Hogan's had a hell of a time lately and our friendship has been tested. I hope when the pressures of today have subsided we will be able to get together and enjoy each other's company away from the cricket field. I asked Martin to be my daughter's godfather, which reflects how I think about him.

My favourite skipper, and the guy for whom leaping off a cliff would have been a pleasure, was John Wright. I guess the main reason I would have been happy to leap off a cliff was that Wrighty would already be halfway down. So many times we'd watch him strap the boards on and face the quicks, never taking a step back – it was compelling viewing, a practical reinforcement of a leader never asking his team to do something he wouldn't do himself.

Wrighty was a man's man, always down to earth, never too complicated and a real straight shooter. Sit him down with a beer, make sure there's a smoker in the group so he can bludge a fag off them, and Wrighty's in his element. A great fund of stories himself, he rewards a good joke with crumple-faced appreciation. At one of my benefit luncheons Wrighty came and spoke for nothing, had the audience in fits and yarned away with my guests for hours afterward which is just typical of the guy.

As a player he became almost reclusive and wrapped himself in a cocoon, so determined was he to play well. One of the few occasions he decided to boof it in a test was against Australia in 1990. On a slow low Basin wicket he carved the Aussies everywhere and demonstrated that along with the dedicated defence and devotion to crease occupation he possessed the full range when it came to shot making. An aggregate of 5000-plus runs puts you in the top echelon of test players the world over and no-one would deny him that status.

I had a word about Franko in the First Class chapter but I would like to talk a bit about him as a New Zealand teammate. Frank had been in the side for about five years when I first made it, often touring as the third opener between Edgar and Wrighty. When he got his chance on a more permanent basis he became a hard guy to shift and always put a heavy price on his wicket. The records will show that he didn't have a prolific test career but what they won't show is the time he spent at the crease taking the sting out of the attack for the guys to follow.

In terms of opening partnerships, Frank and Wrighty have been our most successful combination ever, which begins to demonstrate true worth a little more accurately. There aren't too many thrills and spills with Frank and his choice of career couldn't be more appropriate, the police being lucky to have such a level-headed and able guy in the ranks. The courage he displayed when bouncing back from his airport accident in 1986 was extraordinary and it is puzzling to think he played his last test at the age of 29, particularly given the problems we have had in finding a solid opening combination.

I remember turning up to the airport in 1984, ready to join the Auckland U22 side for the national tournament in Gisborne. Standing in the departure area was a young man wearing a burgundy Lacoste polo shirt, a pencil-thin black leather tie and a pair of mirrored wrap-around sun glasses. To add that he was wearing winklepickers would be embellishment but you can bet your life they weren't Hush Puppies.

That young man was Daniel Kyle Morrison, a loose unit then, who to be honest hasn't done a great deal of tightening since. For that we should all be grateful for he has been a superb cricketer for New Zealand and one of the real characters on and off the track. After a long day in the field you occasionally notice a little change in the run up and before you know it out pops a Malcolm Marshall impression.

Dan's facial expressions are legendary and he is one of the few bowlers in the world who will tap a batsmen on the lid once he's dismissed him. There is a real streak of devilry in him and the only time he seems to get worked up is playing the Pakis – they bring out a bit extra for some reason.

We were having a major leather hunt in Hobart one year when he had Border caught and bowled. (It was his best chance of a catch because we were shelling peas in the grabbers.) Dan's celebration was loud and long, which seemed to upset Border and a bit of banter ensued – I think Dan dismissed him there as well. No-one gives it more than "Deek" and when he's got his rhythm he swings it with more control and pace than most.

The word competitor and John Bracewell are virtually synonymous and we've had some good battles in the past. At Sussex in 1990 I was due to have a rest, having made hundreds in the one-dayers, but Thommo was injured so I had to play, even though I was feeling like an eighty-year-old arthritic. At one stage, when Braces was bowling the ball went past me at cover, so I turned and ran after it, my stiff legs not exactly carrying me at turf-scorching speed. To my horror the batsmen ran four during my chase, and as Hove is not exactly the MCG I realised I had been a tad slow.

My horror was exceeded only by Bracewell's disgust and we soon were having a verbal in the middle of the field. I was knackered and said to Wrighty, "If he goes on like that again I'm gonna punch him." Looking back it's pretty daft, but indicative of how we used to wind each other up.

Now that Braces has retired I have a totally different relationship with him and he has been a big help to me. A few years ago I was having a mid-winter net at Eden Park and popped into Braces' office, asking if I could have a chat for five minutes. An hour later I walked out much the better for his advice and encouragement. He is very good on specifics whereas a lot of coaches tend to be more general, which isn't of great value when you're struggling.

It was my misfortune to enter test cricket at the same time as Jeff Crowe was being shown the exit. Typically, Chopper fought his way back into the side and he was always a great man to have in the dressing room, in the field or at the crease. Much has been said about his high culinary standards and I can vouch for his superior nose for wine, in tastings of which he was always kind enough to include me. The great thing about Chopper was balance – he gave his guts on the track but knew how to enjoy himself away from the game.

There have been numerous discussions about umpires having the power to send dissenting players from the field. I was actually sent from the field early in my career – not for dissent, but for wearing the wrong kit. The sender was not the umpire, but my disgruntled skipper, M.C. Snedden.

Sneds probably thought I was trying to be a bit of a rock star early in my career and when I strolled on to a dampish Eden Park No 2 wearing rubber soles he saw red. I nipped off and changed but I'd made him so livid it was a wee while before I was invited back on the track!

Sneds has always been something of a godfather figure to me – the lawyer, the responsible guy, the fella who loses his constrained demeanour only when he's had a few pots, at which time he takes gibberish to new heights. I am grateful to him as the guy who taught me the ropes in first class and international cricket and it was always a real pleasure taking a catch for him. Taking one for Hadlee, for whom it was day at the office, you'd hear "Taken Paddy" and he was back to his mark.

For Sneds it was different. He sweated blood for every wicket in test cricket and when you helped him snare one it was "Paddy you beauty, yes – YES!" It was great to share his joy, knowing he had been rewarded for all his graft.

We batted together for a long time on two occasions, a couple of left foot left handers, both as boring as each other! I'm sure Sneds will continue to offer plenty to New Zealand cricket – he is such a thorough, well organised, sensible guy and has a heap of good ideas.

When I was first introduced to Stockley Smith, people said, "Be careful of Smithy, he can be a bit moody." It was not a side of him I have particular memories of, but who wouldn't get a bit ratty after keeping for a couple of days with a set of fingers chipped and cracked from hauling in all our wayward returns. When he was fizzing he was unstoppable and he played some fantastic knocks, often when we were knee deep in it. Stockley was very welcoming when I first made the side, which I found great, particularly as he is such a good man socially. Latterly he has made the transition from cricketer to farmer/commentator with ease.

As a keeper, Stockley would stand extraordinarily close to the quicks so that he could take the ball up high – great for him, but it meant the slippers felt a tad close at times!

The catch that was testament to his ability came at Eden Park against Pakistan. Late on the second day, Javed Miandad tried to run Chats fine – being on 271 we thought slips were better deployed elsewhere. In trying to run Chats, Javed didn't get quite enough bat on it but it looked wide enough of Stockley. Unbelievably, after two days with the gloves on, he dived and snapped it up, leaving Miandad gaping.

After we beat India in Bombay, Stockley got up and announced that we were all to report to the team room immediately on our return to the hotel and that no-one would be permitted to leave for a period of five hours. No argument here, Stocks.

Ewen Chatfield had the chance to join the highly paid ranks of professional sport, but turned down Javed Miandad's offer of several million rupees to be a bowling machine in Karachi. Chats was as solid as you can get, Bangalore in 1988 being a notable exception. I think he went through a tour's worth of trousers, but being Chats just kept on running in . . . he kept on running off as well, come to think of it. Having made the mistake early in my career of going for a run with him, I discovered that Chats ran like he bowled – briskish pace and he could go all day!

The heir to the Chatfield throne for some time was the "Auck with the talk", Willie Watson, who apart from being a fine bowler is a very funny guy and a great speaker. Willie would hit the string more than most and was often the victim of an unusual selection policy which saw him missing on wickets that would have really suited him. When he helped bowl the Aussies out at Eden Park in 1993 he showed a glimpse of his real talent, bowling some absolute jaffas.

While not a big drinker, Willie could always sniff out a high quality establishment for a taste or two and was very entertaining company, full of one-liners.

I have mentioned what a privilege it has been to play alongside Richard Hadlee and as a new guy in the team I perceived him as a single-minded, goal-oriented individual who was utterly professional in all he did. Everything he did had a purpose and he liked to be in control. I learnt on an early trip with the New Zealand side just how accurate he liked to be with his life.

I count the tour to India as my first with the New Zealand side but I did take part in a short tour to Sharjah soon after the finish of the domestic season in 1988. As a team we were late for training and as I was last off the bus I suggested to the driver we would be about twenty minutes later than scheduled. I was not on "Time", which is a tour duty designed to make sure buses leave on time and all transport arrangements are in place. Regardless, I thought it was just common sense and went off to training.

I got a bit nervous when I realised training had finished early and the boys started to ask questions like "Where the hell is the bus?" I told the boys what I'd done and a few guys got cabs back but when Paddles turned up the cabs had all gone and he had to wait for the bus, which in the end was very late.

That afternoon Wrighty asked me what had gone on with the buses, as Paddles had had a word to him and was unimpressed, to say the least. I explained what I'd done and said I'd apologised and would do so again at the team meeting if the matter was raised.

Sure enough, Paddles brought it up, saying a few players had been inconvenienced by my actions and that I should be fined! I explained myself again, feeling that things were starting to get a bit silly, and apologised once more, but he wouldn't let go and wanted to fine me. In the end I snapped. "If you're so keen to build team funds," I said, "why don't you chip in." Not surprisingly, this was lead balloon stuff. (Paddles had received some "extras" from one of the sheikhs and it hadn't gone down too well with some of the team.)

I knew I'd overstepped the mark and had to front up and apologise. Thankfully, he took it well, saying he respected me for fronting and speaking my mind, even though he didn't particularly like what I'd said. To him that was the end of it for which I was grateful, because I didn't need him as an enemy that early in my international career. It was only in England in 1990, with his goals behind him and the horizon in sight, that he relaxed and really enjoyed himself off the field and became fun to be around. It was a rare privilege to bat with a knight, which I did for an hour or so at Lord's in the second test.

Andrew Jones, or "Jed" as he was known, was certainly different and I would think not many of the guys he's played cricket with would claim to know him well. Having said that, he was a brilliant competitor with a great record in both test and one-day cricket. There aren't many funny stories about Jed – he was a guy who liked his own space – but to have him at three in your side was a real bonus.

My favourite Jed innings was not one of the seven hundreds he made in test cricket, but it was a hundred for New Zealand. We were lined up against Derby in 1990, against an attack including Malcolm Bishop and another West Indian, Jean-Jacques. Although it was green and hard, Jones just hammered them everywhere, with his trademark back-foot drives racing over the ground. To pick up a hundred against those guys at about a run a ball was a really great knock.

In many ways it was sad that he was recalled and then left out and finished on a bit of a low. It was a no bugles, no drums departure and in many ways typified Jed.

I played a lot for New Zealand with Ken Rutherford, an immensely talented player. It is well documented that his start for New Zealand was a nightmare and it took him a long time to recover. The fact that it took him a longer time than Hogan, who also had a horror start, was basically down to the fact that he was lazy.

It's my belief that, like a lot of talented people, he tried to rely on talent alone and never really put in the hard work that would have given him a solid, rather than a mediocre, test record.

When his game was on song, as it was in the World Cup in 1992 and against the Australians at home the following year, he was great to watch, but they were the only occasions he even began to do justice to his talent.

It is a shame that he has left New Zealand cricket in a bitter frame of mind, and he seems to blame everyone else for his failure . . . looking in the mirror and working hard may answer a few questions for him. In contrast to Willie Watson, he would find a place to drink anywhere – the quality wasn't important as long as the taps were on! If he wanted to, I'm sure he could make enough runs to play for New Zealand again.

My first coach in the New Zealand side was Bob Cunis, who was more often than not hanging off the beige end of a B&H or stretched out having a snooze in the middle of the day. Bob was really from the old school and would tell stories of how in his day you'd charge in all day, give 'em nothing, bowl 35 overs, down 12 beers . . . all that stuff.

A niggly old campaigner, he was very competitive and worked us very hard and loved hitting the high catches, even though he wasn't great at it. There was nothing too complicated in his approach, his philosophy being more about effort and commitment than strategic brilliance. By the time of the England tour in 1990 I think he'd just about had enough and slept for more overs than he watched – more often than not in the team bath.

The tidiest test cricketer I ever played with was Dipak Patel. He was always immaculate and always looked good out in the middle. The 1992 World Cup was his finest moment but he is still playing really well. I've been dropped a few times but Dipper seems to feel the selectors' wrath more than most. It's almost like he's the default option for leaving someone out, but he always bounces back and had a great tour of the West Indies in 1996. I loved touring with him and he was always a good man to share an ale with.

Shane Thomson seems to have picked up a reputation for being a rebel and a bit of a party animal, but when it comes to training or putting in at match-time there aren't many better. The guys call him Arnie because he's always pumping iron and he's certainly bulked up a bit in the last few seasons. Anyone who can swap from being a seamer to a spinner and do it successfully at international level is obviously swamped with talent. Thommo's an interesting guy to tour with and an excellent man on the duty free purchases, particularly on difficult tours.

I loved opening with Rod Latham, mainly because he was one of the few guys I've played with who's got a bigger backside than I have. We must have been quite a sight batting together and could have made a fortune selling billboard advertising on our bums, particularly during the World Cup. The "Roc" is a real Cantab, and sees most things through red and black eyes, but loved playing for New Zealand and made some brilliant contributions, particularly in the one-dayers.

I've spoken about what the loss of Wally Lees is to the game and he was a lovely bloke, tough but always very fair. Wal had an open-door policy during his time as coach and I spent lots of time with him, talking about my game or just about life. He was always very easy to talk to. I thought his real talent was the ability to "know" his players, the ability to know what they really cared about, what they thought about this and that, and how he could use that information to get the best out of players when they were under pressure.

Chris Harris possesses an unbelievable amount of energy and matches it with a great deal of talent. After a super World Cup in 1992 his confidence seemed to wane but a couple of solid years in first class cricket got his game back together. The innings he played against Australia in the latest World Cup quarter-final was delightful to watch, Harry finally demonstrating his full ability on the big stage. Three weeks later he was batting down the list in the West Indies, which certainly had me guessing.

It's everything at speed for Harry and I'm sure he'd love to be a quick, but maybe that wouldn't suit the gentlemanly manner with which he conducts himself. I'm sure Harry's best cricket is ahead of him and I hope he can find a consistent spot in the order before too much longer.

I've got a great deal of admiration for the ability of Dion Nash and his performance at Lord's in 1994 was one that even Paddles would have been proud to put together. Nashy was actually swinging the ball up the slope and had Graham Gooch of all people absolutely on toast. We've had our moments in the past and I think it comes down to both of us being fiercely competitive and giving nothing away on the field. It is a real shame that his 1996 season at Middlesex was fraught with injury, but being a clever guy I'm sure he has continued to learn even when he can't get on the track.

The best of the younger brigade is undoubtedly Stephen Fleming. Flem is one of those infuriating players who just makes the game look easy, and seems to have extra seconds at his disposal, even against the real quicks. It was great to see him pick up a one-day century in the West Indies and I'm sure he will soon start putting together a number of centuries in the longer game.

In some ways it is a shame that he has come into international cricket at such a turbulent time but having survived I'm sure he will enjoy many prosperous years. Flem doesn't have the brashness of some of today's youngsters and is a quality person as well as being a superb player. It wouldn't surprise me if he became a very successful captain in time.

Two or three seasons ago, not many would have picked Nathan Astle to score two hundreds against the Windies and three one-day hundreds in one summer. A bowling all-rounder when he first came into the New Zealand side, he has made a remarkable transformation and his 1995/96 season is the most successful ever by a New Zealand batsman in terms of performance in both forms of cricket. Nathe is a good guy and another who should help form the nucleus of the side for many years.

Chris Pringle, or, as he became known, the "great galah", has paid heavily for his supposed indiscretions, actually missing out on two World Cups. Without question, this would have been hard for him as he is proud to wear the Fern and it is great that he was strong enough to turn his back on the grog and work at his game. I always enjoyed his company and he was a lot of fun to tour with.

The other Chris, Chris Cairns, is undoubtedly one of the best cricketers to play for New Zealand in the past ten years. The huge talent is accompanied by a record that he knows needs to improve if it is truly to reflect the ability. It would be fair to say that until 1995/96 Cairns has shown only glimpses but provided his head stays in the right place I am sure he will entertain crowds and win matches for New Zealand for many years.

It's a long list and there are many more I've taken the field with who haven't been mentioned. I'd like to thank all the guys I've lined up alongside – we've shared some glorious moments and we've had some shockers but I always felt we gave it a hundred and were proud to represent our country.

Pieces in the Puzzle

The New Zealand cricket team is the focal point of the summer game. The players are the people who draw the crowds, provide the thrills and occasion endless debate on the merits of Greatbatch – "He'd never be in my side" – and Pringle – "So what if he enjoys a pint." The players are to the field what actors are to the stage – pretty important in the scheme of things, but useless without good directors, good producers and, dare I say it, good reviews.

The administration of cricket in my time has been a real mixture, consistent with the rapid transformation from game to business. Many of the people who might have thought they had a job for life have been swept aside by the highly professional corporatised approach that is currently being embedded.

Umpires have increasingly become better in New Zealand and internationally the move to neutral umpires has taken some of the doubt out of touring certain countries. Umpire-player relationships are getting better, largely because the standard of umpiring has improved. Confident officials breed confidence in the players, who become less concerned with trying to extract advantage through gamesmanship.

I've always had a good relationship with the media, believing that being honest and available has its rewards. For those in sport who don't like what the press has to say, the remedy is simple – don't read the papers. The majority of guys involved with reporting cricket in this country are honest guys who have no need to stoop to sensationalism. Besides, if any player thinks it's rough here, try having a turn in England!

The characters who follow are those who have been in the game during my career and who have had an impact or made an impression.

Graham Dowling was at the helm when I first came into international cricket. Graham was a sincere man but liked to be distant from his players. I understand he used to negotiate well with other countries in terms of filling up our international calendar, but he was very much an "us and them" type in terms of the administrator-player relationship.

The transformation in his role to what it has become today was rapid and I think he moved out at an appropriate time. When Peter McDermott became chairman, Graham's influence began to wane and it became increasingly difficult to get a decision out of NZC over even the most trivial matter.

Peter McDermott took over New Zealand cricket and I mean he *took over* New Zealand Cricket. Instead of running his board, which is the chairman's usual brief, Peter decided to do the chief executive's job and all manner of other roles, eventually enjoying more publicity than the respective captains of the day.

Everything had to go through Peter, which cluttered decision-making and left many NZC staff disillusioned. It was as if this was his moment in the sun and he was going to enjoy his high profile to the max. If he felt that there was a dearth of competence running the game, his role was to improve that situation, not run the game himself.

In his defence, he must have felt he was dealing with

some pretty amateurish performers if our experience in England in 1994 is anything to go by. When approached by British Telecom, who wanted to use the team to encourage Kiwis to call home, Mike Sandlant contacted New Zealand Cricket. The marketing manager of the time suggested we ask for $3000! We were paid £16,000 and I reckon that was still pretty cheap for them.

I have talked about Peter's role in Sri Lanka and I stress the invidiousness of his position, but his work there was not conducted along lines of strict honesty or integrity. That tour was going to happen even if he had to roll a couple of left arm spinners over himself, and his behaviour reflected this.

The money handed to people that he really had no right to approve has been staggering, and there is even a suggestion of mis-information in some of his dealings with his own board.

Andrew Jones has been among the highest paid players in New Zealand cricket in the last eighteen months or so, and yet he hasn't played since the West Indies were here in 1995. I have nothing against Jones being well paid if he is performing for New Zealand but for someone to be paid while sitting on the farm in Wanganui is unbelievably wasteful. The board were informed that Jones' contract appeared large because of a performance component – that component never existed. And the Jones contract was small beer when lined up alongside the payment made to Geoff Howarth.

Howarth had failed in many elements of his role yet McDermott saw fit to authorise a six-figure handshake substantially above that authorised by the board. Imagine the development that sort of money could achieve if shared among the respective cricket associations, rather than lining the pockets of a man whose culpability in the near-death of New Zealand cricket in the time he was in charge was enormous.

The lawyers who represented Howarth clearly

outmuscled McDermott and his legal team, because buying his silence for a period of two years is nonsense. The damage they were scared of then is just as real now, if it were real in the first place.

After the success of the 1992 World Cup the players' committee proposed a small increase in match fees. We were laughed at. There was no thought of a bonus and yet for many players who had yet to be contracted (at that stage me among them) uncertainty remained. No financial incentive to succeed, but obvious financial penalties for failure – I'm sure most employees would find such a situation untenable.

I guess my main problem with Peter McDermott was his insistence on prefacing all his conversations with "You know me, you can trust me". I was waiting for "Have I got a deal for you".

Unfortunately, when he did have a deal for me it was presented in fairly bizarre circumstances. A meeting was arranged for Peter McDermott, Graham Dowling, my manager and myself to discuss the terms of my contract with New Zealand Cricket. When we sat down McDermott's first words were, "Here's the contract, it's not negotiable – take it or leave it." The point of Dowling flying up from Christchurch for that sort of meeting still escapes me.

The monthly payments were based on the cricket that was scheduled, plus a small premium for my perceived worth to New Zealand cricket. One of the more bizarre elements was a clause allowing for additional payments if more one-dayers were scheduled but if there were more test matches that was hard luck. When I asked why, I was told that New Zealand Cricket made no money out of tests and couldn't afford to pay any extra! Effectively they were asking me to play for free in any unscheduled test matches, which I found bewildering.

As his crowning achievement, McDermott presided over the re-appointment of Glenn Turner, a man who had done the job before and had been found wanting in terms of man-management. There is no doubt some disciplines had to be instilled but the fact that the past is the best predictor of future performance was proved yet again.

Grenville Alabaster, the southern schoolmaster, was an interesting mix. Like Turner, he recognised the need for some discipline but by the end of the Indian tour in 1995 he was becoming petty. Managing a New Zealand cricket team involves dealing with individuals under varying amounts of pressure and individuals with different levels of respect for authority. Gren was a genuine guy but he tended to think anyone asking a question was undermining his authority and he lacked the essential people skills in terms of treating people as individuals and indeed respecting that individuality. I actually enjoyed talking cricket with him but that was not his role on tour and he seemed to try and impose that side of himself on us, possibly to try and mask his management shortcomings. I guess Gren was doing the best job he could but I think he forgot all about the enjoyment factor which is especially crucial in places like India.

One manager who could relate was Ian "Dicky Ticker" Taylor, so named for his heart palpitations during the riot in Peshawar – things were a bit serious and good old Frank had to stay behind because Ian was too crook to travel with the team. Ian was one of the open-door type managers. You would feel very comfortable about popping into his room and having a chat, whether it concerned tour matters or just for a yarn. Ian knew about people and worked hard for the players; and although he was very familiar with the players we all knew he was in charge and respected him immensely.

The fact that players have gone to visit Ian since he stood down from the post says much for his standing with the team. He was in stark contrast to Gerad Bailey, who, although a nice guy, was the classic "spend time on the board and we'll give you a tour" type manager.

If you wanted to write a fictional tale outlining a manager's worst nightmare, you'd be hard pressed to top having a captain at loggerheads with the opposition administration and the team caught up in the middle of a bomb scare. Leif Dearsley copped both in his time in the job and they were both on the same tour! Leif was my former boss at Lion Breweries and I was always impressed by his organisational skills and his ability to get things done for the players.

Hogan had a major axe to grind with the Zimbabwean officials about match conditions and suchlike, which stretched Leif's diplomacy skills to the limit. I thought he did well given his multiple responsibilities as manager and representative of New Zealand Cricket. But that stuff and nonsense was reduced to trivia in the face of the bomb in Sri Lanka. Unfortunately, Leif was told initially that the players' wishes would be complied with but McDermott's arrival meant all that was going to change. Leif was put in the embarrassing position, through no fault of his own, of having to alter his position. As the point of contact for the board and the players, he became the meat in a pretty ordinary sandwich.

Leif is a big supporter of cricket and loves the game in the same way that Alabaster and Taylor do – I hope his view hasn't been altered by his experiences on that tour.

The only failing of Mike Sandlant was that he was too nice a guy – so nice he gave Geoff Howarth a couple of favourable reports about his tour performances, which probably kept him in the job. Mike was a capable manager who cared about his players, and as a proud New Zealander it was a shame he was involved in such a distasteful period in New Zealand cricket.

Umpires are a different breed all right. I mean, who else would stand out in the middle all day, the target of player and spectator inquisition alike, and yet still pride themselves on maintaining their equilibrium and being accurate right up to the last ball of the day? I enjoy having a chat with the umpires – it's relaxing when you're batting and provides an interesting diversion when fielding. There's nothing like a chat with David Shepherd when someone is blocking the poop out of it over after over, or watching Dickie Bird's antics as he twitches his way through the day.

I definitely got off on the wrong foot with Steve Dunne, which is not clever for any player. We had a definite disconnect in terms of the LBW law, largely at my expense. As a former left arm seamer I think he was trying to make up for all the ones he didn't get as a bowler! Steve and I get on well now but I still like to play as many as I can when he's down the other end – that's my problem though, as Steve is a very good umpire and has earned the respect of players around the world.

Brian Aldridge has always impressed me as a totally unshakeable individual who put up with a lot and still retained his composure. In my first game at Lancaster Park, Sneds thought he had Dayle Hadlee in front and appealed with some certainty – he was a brave man to turn Sneds down but it was at Lancaster Park!

Sneds was nothing compared to Salim Malik in a one-dayer a few years later. Saleem Jaffer (and he bowled the odd one) got one through Hogan and the Pakistanis went up to a man. Aldridge turned the appeal down and from then on Malik, who evidently had a super view from point, proceeded to taunt Aldridge after each delivery – "Aldridge you are a f—ing cheat" time and time again. I suggested to Brian that he should take some action but he just shrugged his shoulders and said, "These guys are like this a bit." Despite the Pakistanis' attitude, Brian is another New Zealand umpire well respected by opposition teams.

Lambton Square grocer Steve Woodward was involved a lot early in my career and he, too, took plenty of stick from the Pakistanis. Every now and then the glasses would start to twitch a bit, but he was generally very composed. The best thing about Steve was his ability to leave things on the field – he had a real understanding of competitive situations and how they affect players, so he didn't take too much to heart. Having said that, I don't think he sends many

Christmas cards to Faisalabad.

I'm always called portly or rotund so I don't feel too bad about describing David Shepherd in this vein. There's no doubt he's a popular man among the catering staff around the world and I've had the sobering experience of watching him annihilate a serving of lunch at Lord's. The food there will never get a mention in a Healthy Heart book and Shep just murdered a big plate of chops, gravy, buttered potatoes and peas.

Fielding is a part of the game I try very hard to enjoy and be involved in but when it gets a little tiring David is the best sort of tonic to get you moving again. As umpires go, he's one of the best in terms of having respect from the players without ever having to resort to admonishment. If ever a problem appears to be brewing he seems to be able to sort it out with the player rather than having to call in the captain, which immediately draws attention to what is often a heat-of-the-moment issue.

On the other end of the scale is Khizer Hayat, who gives the distinct impression of having no idea. We met him at a function in Pakistan and he was most offended he hadn't been asked to officiate in the tests. When you tour Pakistan they give you a list of umpires from which to choose; a bit like selecting which way you are going to die. The infamous Shakoor Rana was also on the list and I think he and Khizer were the first names scratched – it's almost a case of the devil you don't know. Khizer was extremely miffed and probably can't wait to fire the boys out next time they front.

Being an umpire in Pakistan is a big deal and they appear very proud of their status in the game. If cricket statistics were kept like basketball's, they would top the list for assists; but to be fair, they are subject to enormous pressure and their Home and Contents premiums must be enormous!

Jack Hampshire was another of the English umpires who have played test cricket and knows the game inside out. Jack is a real hard shot and stands no nonsense on the field. When the big Yorkshire accent booms "pull your head in lud" not many guys argue. Now that he is taking over as coach of Zimbabwe, I'm sure he'll provide a huge boost for their cricket but it's a shame to see such a good umpire leaving the test panel.

No section on umpires could finish without mention of the greatest of them all, "Dickie" Bird. Although as mad as a snake, he is a tremendous guy and just eats, breathes and sleeps the game. In one of the test matches in Zimbabwe he got an attack of the runs and he started to make for the pavilion with an "Ahm not too good 'ere luds – Ahm off!" At times he was almost apologetic about giving guys out – "Sorry lud. Ah've got ta give that" – which was partially consoling for a batsman.

My dealings with the media have been more about having a beer on tour than any great drama with what they've written about me. Eric "Egg Foo" Young was about when I was first getting going and he gave me some pretty good press early on. Eric was always a good tourist, with a distinct feel for the finer things in life.

Don Cameron has been a great supporter and has written kindly of me when I've been out of nick. Often guys can't wait to see you fall but I always felt Don was really hoping I would succeed – maybe so he could give full range to his descriptive techniques! I think the important thing with Don was you could have a beer with him confident that what you said was not going to be all over the *Herald* the next day.

Of the other scribes, David Leggat of NZPA was always a good man to have around and he seemed to really enjoy what he was doing, which I think reflected the way he wrote about us. And Peter Bidwell has been pretty good to me – honest when I'm out of nick but always supportive.

The radio guys are anchored by Brian Waddle, a larrikin of the first order but an excellent broadcaster. The tales of Waddle on tour are legendary and as a practical joker it is always nice to get one back on him. Unfortunately in 1990 it nearly backfired on us. At a function in Pakistan (there seem to be lots of them) we ran a couple of party games on the lawn for a bit of a diversion, including the old fashioned egg and spoon race.

As Wads was running backwards, cradling his egg, one of the guys stuck out a leg and down he went. When his head hit the ground it was like a gun going off. He lay there dazed for a moment, before getting up and going absolutely spare – "If I find out who did that . . ." Once we knew he was OK we just fell about, knowing of course that Wads would be back.

Wads has been touring with New Zealand sides for many years and it will be a big loss for the game when he switches off the mike.

The other pieces in the puzzle are integral to the game and it's important that everyone understands the role they play in bringing the game to the public. There have been too many instances of all the pieces being pushed in different directions at various times in my career. I hope that once the new administration is fully operational we will all be focused on delivering good cricket. The players playing well within a structure competently administered, the umpires calling it accurately and the media reporting honestly but positively. A year or two ago that sort of scenario had as much chance of happening as a general issue of Swanndris in Hell, but I'm sure we are moving rapidly in the right direction.

It's Not All Bouncers and Broken Fingers

Among the genuine perks involved in being a test cricketer are the opportunities that become available for travel, for unique experiences and, of course, the ability to make money doing something you love. Tours with New Zealand teams offer two choices; stay in your room and watch *Die Hard* eight times, or get out and soak up the country as much as you can. Almost without exception people are proud to show you their country and the things that make it different and have always enjoyed adding to my list of life experiences.

I've been rewarded for giving it a bit of a nudge at the start of the innings by numerous invitations to play benefit matches or charity games. Often charities will pick a World XI, which doesn't mean the best players in the world, merely an assortment of available test cricketers from around the world. The usual pre-requisite is the ability to boof it, as punters turn up at these matches expecting to be entertained. Following, in no particular order, are some of the interesting times I have been lucky enough to have experienced.

Whenever a New Zealand side visits England, a little

trip across the Irish Sea is part of the itinerary. On our 1990 excursion we were welcomed at a function in Northern Ireland in what we were to learn later was the "most bombed hotel in the world" . . . ironic, given my experiences to follow in Sri Lanka. Incidentally, the hotel has finally succumbed to the constant barrage and no longer exists.

Anyway, at the function a couple of gents starting talking to us about golf and would we like a game at Royal County Down. Jeff Crowe's ears really pricked up as County Down is one of the great courses in world terms and we were soon arranging one of the matches off so we could play. After completing twelfth man duties in the morning we met the two gents for lunch at the club. Caddies were arranged for us, but one of the men took us aside and mentioned that if we wanted to discuss the situation in Ireland we would be better to do it out of earshot of the caddies. Apparently, they were from areas which were IRA strongholds and any opinion on the situation may not have been that welcome.

Unfortunately, after about twelve holes the rain came down in a big way, so much so that we had to tee the ball on the fairway and putting was out of the question.

When we came in from the round two baths were run for us and a pint of Guinness and a tumbler of whiskey was brought down to warm us up. When changed we wandered upstairs to the lovely old lounge for a bit of "crack" over another pint of Guinness. The hospitality was superb and the day ended too soon as we had to be at an official function. We arrived early at the function and Ireland being the security conscious place that it is we didn't have a prayer of being let in without some form of official pass. Luckily, there was a nice little local nearby . . .

Every year the Princes Trust Charity has a series of events to raise money for various causes. One year I was invited to take part in a day where the day's entertainment was a cricket match and the evening's entertainment was a rock concert. Competing in the match were the likes of

Allan Border, Martin Crowe, Imran Khan, Carl Hooper and David Gower, while the rock concert featured Van Morrison, Swing Out Sister, Nigel Kennedy, John Farnham, Spandau Ballet and Level 42.

Naturally, the artists came and watched the cricket and we got to see the concert, which was superb, each artist singing a couple of songs and handing on to the next act. I met Prince Charles after the game when all the players were presented with an engraved crystal decanter as a memento of the occasion. I still had a zinc-covered nose when I went up which seemed to amuse him and I hope he didn't think I was being smart when I told him I had a whole potful in the dressing room. I wasn't meaning he'd need it to cover his snorer . . . It was great talking to the music stars afterward, with people like Tony Hadley of Spandau Ballet being as interested in our profession as we were in theirs.

A number of musicians in England are in love with cricket and Eric Clapton even has his own XI. I played in a game with Bill Wyman and Eric Clapton and it was funny being in a cricket dressing room with girls calling out your teammates' names. I told Bill that there were few girls out there who seemed keen to meet him but he said it was pretty quiet compared to his days with the Stones.

Looking at his face was like a peek into a museum of one vice or another. Dennis "Minder" Waterman was another in that side, also a great bloke, but he, too, had been round the clock a couple of times.

I was asked to play in a single-wicket competition as part of the Newcastle Garden Festival. Gooch and Hick of England, Marshall of the West Indies, Shastri of India and Batchy from New Zealand! With £30,000 prize money on offer – an amazing amount of money to be playing for – the day was made definitely more relaxing by a little agreement among the players before the game. When I looked at the calibre in the room I said deal me in sharply. I was confident of giving it a nudge but my little leggers might have gone a long way in that company.

The annual Jesmond Festival is always a good one to be involved in as the players are asked to an old estate named Linden Hall. The place is now an hotel and everything is done in fine English tradition. All the staff are given photos of the players and strict instructions to meet every need. The cellar is a sensation and there aren't too many in the world who would grumble at the wine list.

I've always been fascinated by South Africa and accordingly leapt at the chance to visit when invited to Kepler Wessels' benefit series. Dipak and I were the Kiwi contingent and it was great to line up with Geoff Marsh, Aravinda, Otis Gibson and Tom Moody.

We were in pre-season mode so were determined to get in as much fitness as possible. Choosing Geoff Marsh as a running mate proved brave, but foolish, as he set preposterous standards in terms of speed and distance. When we wandered out for our first hit on grass I told Swampy I'd take first hit – not clever. Forty yards away and beginning the charge was Schulz, the big left armer, and he was extra quick. I survived the first over only to be greeted by Swampy grinning widely asking innocently, "How are things at your end?" Not surprisingly, I was out soon after, playing what I thought was a perfectly good forward defence only to discover my off stump was still in the ground but ten yards away from where it should have been.

My only other experience of the republic was with David Hookes and Martin Crowe for what can only be described as a sort of airlines corporate six-a-side. The tournament itself wasn't that well organised but the golf was perfect and we made the most of that. We were taken out to Sun City which is effectively four hotels, two golf courses – one having a crocodile pit to the left of the fourth fairway; don't bother looking for lost balls there – and a casino.

A day and a night at Kruger Park was a magic time, highlighted by spotting a pack of wild dogs. This would not be notable had it not been for the reaction of the ranger who was very excited saying how rare it was to see it.

Greatbatch Collection

The boundary hunter in relax mode.

Floating on air in my first test knock – I was soon back down to earth.

J.G. Blackwell

In line and dropping the gloves – that's the way!

Over page: Lining up with a few legends. (Greatbatch Collection)

GEORGE
1851
BY
IN RECOGNITION
RENDERED TO
A PERIOD OF
AND A WISE

ORY OF
ANNING
RIS 1932
SERVICES
LUB OVER
S HE WAS
NTLEMAN
HOSE
WANED

The Bradford lads in 1982 – I've either got two sweaters on or a weight problem.

Suburban Newspapers Limited

One there Roc – a rare single v South Africa.

J.G. Blackwell

Dancing down to Akram – good idea Paddy.

With Marina and baby Alice, at home in Hawke's Bay.

Apparently the dogs scare the hell out of the hyenas and when it's one on one the hyenas don't want to know.

At the end of the trip, Jo'burg lived up to its burgeoning reputation as the crime capital of the world. We returned from golf to find Hooksey's hotel room door was missing – no subtlety of method here, just off with the door and grab all you can carry. As it happens that was everything Hooksey had, which put a dampener on the visit.

Perhaps the most interesting venue I've ever taken guard in was the Skydome in Toronto. Another "World XI" was assembled to take on the West Indies, on a wicket which was artificial turf on wooden boards – did it skid on! As we approached the stadium it became apparent that parking was underneath and we parked the car and took the lift to the second floor – our dressing room. We weren't allowed into the Bluejays' dressing room which was disappointing, but just being in that stadium was a tremendous experience.

On the surface, Toronto seems a somewhat incongruous venue for a cricket match, but it is a very cosmopolitan city and about 20,000 turned up, largely Asians, West Indians and ex-pats. I went directly from Toronto to the Melbourne Cup which put paid to my match fee in no time!

Pakistan is a country where popping down to your local for a pint usually means visiting Ranjiva, the village goat, for your ration of milk. Not so for the rich and famous, as I was to discover on our 1990 tour.

Javed Miandad had promised to take me out for a night, which I thought would be a bit of fun and I waited eagerly to hear the arrangements. We were at Karachi, a coastal city, when I got the call, and the invitation to bring a couple of mates. Frank and Dipper were keen so we went as instructed up to Javed's room. Or should I say rooms, for when we got there we discovered that the captain of Pakistan had two rooms, one for him and one for entertaining. The entertainment room was also where his minder slept – his minder!

The room was full of people from all over the world

and we had a drink and a chat there before being picked up outside the lobby by a couple of limousines. Things were going pretty well and we soon found ourselves at the Karachi version of Westhaven – we were off for a sail!

A kilometre or two offshore we boarded another boat, a huge old schooner with a large entertainment area on the foredeck. In the middle of the deck was a low table covered in cold Heinekens, numerous varieties of Scotch and assorted other beverages. Frank and Dipper were feeling pretty good about coming along and I was pretty fired up myself.

Another boat arrived and off hopped the entertainment for the evening – dancing girls. Yes, the genuine article, and they kept their veils on. It was clear that appreciation was registered by tossing the average annual income into the middle and wads of rupees inches thick were thrown in – there was no call for my loose change.

After the dancing another boat turned up and Frank was delirious to discover it was feast time – food of every description and some that defied it was placed in front of us. Seafood is a big no no on tours of the sub-continent and we considered the matter carefully in the face of the king prawns in front of us. "We're not having fish are we lads?" "No, not us." . . . "Out of my way!" It was, in my experience, one of the great banquets– Javed had spared nothing – and something of an eye-opener to see the number of people on board from a variety of different cultures enjoying the festivities for what was clearly not the first time.

The evening looked like a potential disaster when a navy patrol boat turned up looking like it was keen to investigate proceedings. Javed grabbed a couple of bottles of Scotch, leapt aboard, had a yarn to the captain and before we knew it the boat had vanished. "Cricketers as gods" before our eyes.

The other side of Pakistan was evidenced when we went up to the Afghanistan border, under police escort, to see the freedom fighters. It was eerie seeing the burnt-out Russian tanks just lying around as relics or being used as target practice by the youthful trainees. We could hear all manner of weaponry going off beyond the first hills and the police told us it was indeed practice. There, a young kid's idea of a "net" is to fire off a few bazookas with his mates. We were able to visit this area as we were in the district to play a one-dayer at Arbab Niaz stadium in Peshawar – a game of cricket cheek by jowl with violence and unrest.

Experiencing a riot was something none of us had included in our tour goals. As we drove into Peshawar, a town that looked like something out of the 'thirties (you can read that as the 1930s or the 1530s), things were not a hundred. Riots had slowed the highway to a walk and I nipped up onto the roof of the bus to capture some of the proceedings – a little wave of a machine gun convinced me that back in the bus was my best bet, and we eventually made it to the ground in time for quick warm-ups and the start of the match.

Unfortunately our performance won't make any "What Happened Next" videos as typically for that tour we made bugger-all and Waqar got five for. As the Pakistanis cruised to a win the crowd felt they'd been short-changed and started firing objects on to the field. I was at mid-on and got nailed by a big piece of brick, which drew a bit of claret. Hogan saw the damage and hauled us off as Intikhab walked around the ground trying to placate the multitudes. I don't think the message was getting through because in the best traditions of Stamford Bridge the crowd were ripping up their seats and firing them into the middle.

We were unamused and unconvinced when he came in and said, "I've sorted it out now." Good one Inti. Finally, we went back on but all stood at the tunnel end of the ground for the last ball and jetted off the field, still earning a shower of debris for our trouble. Although we stayed in the dressing room for an hour or so afterwards there were still plenty of them waiting for us when we left and I can safely say that whoever held the debris concession in Peshawar was the only one smiling at the end of that debacle.

On a more pleasant note, Mudassar Nazar took me out to visit Hanif Mohammed (he had a pretty fair grog cabinet too) and it was great to chat with one of the game's legends. Hanif was a charming old guy and was genuinely interested in developments in New Zealand cricket and what was being done for our young players. Shaoib, his son, was hitting us everywhere and he was obviously very proud.

Early in 1991, Ian Mune approached me to play W.G. Grace in a movie, *The End of the Golden Weather*. I was to be in the protagonist's dream as he went from eating an apple to running in and bowling it to the legendary WG; the scene involved me lofting one and being caught. I asked if I needed to put on any weight for the role in true De Niro style, but they thought I was fine as I was! Unfortunately, I got a shattering call from Ian saying that time constraints on the movie meant I was on the cutting room floor – the Hollywood dream was over.

I've always admired golfers for their ability to concentrate and perform under pressure. In 1989, Hogan and I went to the British Open at Troon determined to get close to the action. We had tickets for every day and on the third day a guy came up and offered to sell us a "Quiet Please" sign and a steward's badge. The sign had been autographed by many of the players so it had some souvenir value, but our plans were far more cunning.

The guy had been a steward on the fourth hole and the equipment was marked accordingly but we decided to have a crack at being stewards at every hole, figuring that if we looked confident we could get close to the golfers without causing anyone any grief. The plan was going perfectly until some eagle-eyed official spotted us on the ninth, but instead of reprimanding us he just said, "Back to your hole please."

On the morning of the final round, Greg Norman predicted he would need to shoot 63 to win the golf tournament. He shot 64 and a play-off was on. We watched him birdie the first six holes of the day and it was like watching golf from another planet. We were determined to be up close for the play-off which featured Norman, fellow Australian Wayne Grady and the American Mark Calcavecchia.

Hogan knew one of the guys at Australia's Channel 7 and he managed to get us crew passes for the play-off, which meant we could walk up the fairways with the players, an astonishing privilege and one we enjoyed for three holes before a guy tapped me on the shoulder and asked what I was doing. I handed him my pass and said I was part of the crew. His reply was instant. "No you're not – off the course now!" I was happy to go, having exceeded all expectations of the experience, and was still close enough when Calcavecchia sealed it.

After the Perth test in 1989 a few of the guys were invited for a sail on the Whitbread boat *Fisher & Paykel.* Grant Dalton showed us a few of the ropes and out we went, into the big swells off Fremantle – well they were big enough for Stockley and me although the Whitbread boys probably thought they were becalmed. I took the helm for a while and I guess we were pretty lucky to get back in but it was an exciting experience and a taste of the sort of things the Whitbread guys do for weeks on end.

When we got back to land we sat down to big load of fish and chips and it was great to yarn to the crew about their experiences at sea. It is always nice to talk to top sportsmen about the challenges they face – they made my marathon seem pretty short!

A visit to South Australia always promised much more than a game of cricket. In the cricket match, Hogan would get a ton; after the cricket match, Chopper would lead a visit to the Yalumba winery, in the fabled Barossa Valley.

After one great tour of the vineyard and wine making area we headed to the boardroom where our host, Peter Sawrey, pulled out a case of cold beer! "We were actually a bit keener on a tasting thanks Pete!" The man has wine day in day out and was keen on a beer, but he duly obliged and we were educated on a number of his finest. For lunch we popped out to a magnificent area overlooking a lake to enjoy a huge picnic, helped along by some fantastic wine.

Having been hosted so magnificently, it would have been rude not to have gone into the local village of Angaston for a cleanser. It was pleasant chatting to the locals, the vast majority of whom are immersed in the wine industry. Feeling pretty immersed ourselves, we headed back to the hotel having enjoyed a superb day, with only the driver remaining awake for the two-hour journey.

Apart from all the great things I've received as an international cricketer, it's also nice to be involved in the giving side as well. I have been fortunate to be asked to a number of schools to talk to the youngsters about FairPlay or just about playing cricket for New Zealand. It is very rewarding and I hope some of the children will want to be involved in cricket, or any sport, as a result.

Charity functions are usually a lot of fun and you get to meet other New Zealand sportsmen and women and a few "proper" celebrities as well.

My most memorable occasion was a weekend of fundraising for Ronald McDonald House in Wellington. Causes like this are so essential, it is a real pleasure to be involved, but they make you work for the money you raise! The evening started with trips around Wellington's pubs, just handing around a bucket for the punters to fill up, but also auctioning off kisses from the stars and that sort of thing. After Commonwealth Games boxer Mike Kenny was auctioned off lock, stock and barrel, we didn't see him again. Now that I think of it, I haven't seen him since! Hope you're OK Mike.

Anyway, this went on for a while until Philip Rush had to leave to prepare for a swim from Petone to Oriental Bay. It was the middle of winter and we wished him luck but thought we'd stick with the support boat. Two hundred metres from shore Jock Hobbs and I had a rush of blood and it was down to the undies and into the tide to help

Rushy with the final few metres. I felt like the guy who came second in the Cold Power ad but eventually made it to shore with a very relaxed Philip Rush and a very cold Jock Hobbs and the crowd gave us a warm round of applause as we stumbled up the beach. We raised a fair chunk of money for the House and it was a great opportunity to use my "status" positively for the benefit of sick kids and their families.

I've tried to take every opportunity going as an international cricketer. It has been great to enjoy so many different experiences but also to talk to other New Zealand sportsmen about their challenges. New Zealand representatives all share a common bond and even if you haven't met someone from another code it is easy to strike up a conversation.

Going out on the Whitbread boat is a classic example of being able to really share ideas on sport in general rather than being code-specific. I wouldn't expect Raw Meat Taylor to come and have a net at Lord's before a test match and he wouldn't see the funny side of me going for a sail the day before the Whitbread fleet was due to leave. But when the time is right I'd be happy to put him in front of the bowling machine and let him face a few deliveries at 90 miles an hour – just to say thanks!

Foe or Friend

Cricket affords wonderful opportunities to meet your opposition, to share a drink and reflect on the events of the day. Regrettably, many players shun the opportunity and they, and the game, are the poorer for it. Some teams actively discourage the practice, suggesting it might take the edge from their play. I've had the odd dressing room beer with Merv Hughes and it didn't seem to change his approach once he stepped over the boundary rope.

Very few professions create an environment where friendships and contacts on a global scale are so easy to make and where possible I have grabbed the chance to talk to the opposition, to hear their thoughts on the game and on the country they represent. I consider myself fortunate to have made some great friends among the test players of the world and also to have pitted myself against some of the game's legends.

The Australians are a side I love playing against and I always lifted my intensity when it came to Allan Border. For some reason I was like red rag to a bull and his "Mr Grumpy" tag would surface soon after I took guard. We faced a smallish second innings total to win the third test in 1993 but often those smallish totals can mess you up if you try to play too cautiously. I plumped for the other end of the scale and started dancing down the wicket and flaying at anything in my half. In the dressing room afterward Border just looked at me and said, "Gee Paddy, when you lose it, you really do lose it don't you!"

In Sydney in 1994, when the New Zealand team became a little over-aggressive in an effort to show that we weren't going to lie down, we were amazed to see him complain about us in the morning papers – we were just taking a leaf out of the Border book! A 10,000 run, 150 test career says it all for his ability, his stamina and his will to win. He's a great cricketer and one I'm grateful I got the opportunity to compete against.

One of the toughest guys I ever played was David "Babs" Boon. Babs doesn't say a great deal but you can bet your life he's going to sell his wicket only to the very highest bidder. I have been lucky enough to have a few good chats with him about my game and he once informed me that I was a good player and didn't need to overdo the aggression on the field. It was a message delivered with sincerity and I certainly took it on board. I took him and Ian Healy up to the Gluepot one night to listen to a bit of music, and Boony demonstrated that his legendary love of a taste is not just myth.

A night out with Ian Healy means there will never be a lull in the conversation. On the field, in tandem with Warne, he is the Energiser man; never stops talking. "Bowling Warney", "He doesn't know which way it's going mate" and the default call "bowled Shane" just go on and on. Heals is a very open guy and loves a chat about the game. I was amazed at his admission after the Perth test in 1989 that he thought he might be dropped, his record since demonstrating that his fears were without foundation.

A man Kiwis love to hate is Dean Jones, and getting him out was always a special moment. I'd known him for many years after playing cricket in the Yorkshire leagues, but when we got out on the field internationally it was war. For a while he would barely acknowledge us and we suspected Bobby Simpson may have felt it didn't suit Deano's mental approach if he was too close to the opposition.

Only in Darwin as recently as last year did he relax and relate and he treated Hogan and I like long lost friends. It is amazing that a guy with a one-day average over fifty and a test average in the mid-forties has failed to make a full comeback to the Australian side.

I'd like to say that Merv Hughes is just a big fat Australian but unfortunately he's a lot more than that . . . besides, he might read this one day. Merv is just a big kid who loves a practical joke, but will do anything to get you out once he's got the ball in hand. I've experienced both sides of Merv in quick succession, at Eden Park in 1993. It was the afternoon I went ballistic and Merv didn't see the funny side, to the point of sending a bit of saliva Batchward. I can still remember his dodgy breath, which gives you an indication of how close he was and if it was within the rules to get physical Merv would have been into it.

The next day, with the test won, Merv proceeded to mimic my knock, bum out, mouthing Watch the Ball, the full works – it was a remarkable resemblance if you disregard his girth and a nice indication that he could leave it on the field, which a few players struggle to do.

I've enjoyed some great moments against England and I've also had some lows. One guy who has been a good friend throughout has been Robin Smith. Nicknamed "the Judge" because of his judicial mane of hair, Robin Smith would count as my closest mate in international cricket. We correspond frequently and it is always a pleasure to play against the guy. It is not unusual for him to wander past in a test and say "you're playing well today Batchy", which displays a good sense of balance in his approach to the game. This does not suggest any lack of hardness and his record against the West Indies is testimony to his mental strength. The way he bashed us around Headingly in 1990 shows he's not short of physical strength either, and it is puzzling that the England selectors do not always consider him a certainty for their side.

A cry of "Batchy, howsit man" can mean only one thing – Allan "Legga" Lamb is around. Actually it means two things, the other being that I will soon be enjoying a beverage of some sort. Lamb lives life at a million miles and hour and the few days I had playing in benefit matches with him were some of the most exhausting of my life. Like the Judge, Legga has a remarkable record against the quicks and like many of the greats seems to have an extra second with which to play the ball.

I didn't play a lot against Beefy Botham but I include him in this list because he was out on his own when it came to inner belief. Sometimes he thought he was bulletproof but in terms of representing attitude on a sportsfield Botham was second to none. Like Merv Hughes, Both just wanted to have fun and he certainly "lived" life – there was no way he was ever going to die wondering. In the end his self-belief probably led to him playing a season too long, but even in his final year he felt he was good enough to take on the Aussies.

Gladstone Small is a lovely guy and his characteristic "no-neck" run up makes him stand out. There are guys who are quicker, but he bowls a very "hard" ball, always hitting the bat. Gladdy has usually got a set of golf clubs over his shoulder and is absolutely fanatical about the game – he'll play anywhere, anytime.

The Indians are by and large the gentlemen of international cricket and none fits this tag better than Mohammed Azharuddin. When he bashed us at Baroda we could have had twenty in the field and he still would have dominated us, so cleanly did he hit the ball. In India in 1995 he went out of his way to look after us and was very hospitable. Reebok signed Azza just before the tour and everywhere we went we saw Reebok shoes the size of a car and Azza's new Mercedes on display, side by side. It turned out that Azza's brother was driving the car from venue to venue, quite a feat on the roads of India.

If ever a sobriquet was appropriate, it's the tagging of Sachin Tendulkar as the baby-faced assassin. Sachin is a very well mannered, very softly spoken individual, to the point where you have to lean a bit closer when you're talking to him. At the moment he punches out three-hour hundreds and it will be interesting to see how many he gets the first time he bats for a day and a half.

Much is made of Sachin's superstar status in India and in 1995 we experienced it first hand. Heading for the first one-dayer, we had to go to the Calcutta train station. As we pulled up to the station we were surrounded by 10,000 fans (the Indian bus was beside ours), all striving for a glance at their heroes. The two teams were escorted to the trains by rows and rows of the local constabulary and although it was reassuring it didn't exactly feel safe. As we made our way down the platform we realised the line had been breached and hundreds of fans were streaming down the platform chasing Sachin, wanting to touch him or get a photo. The Indians looked at us and said "run" and we were relieved to get on the train and the hell out of Calcutta.

Sachin at age twenty-four has at least another decade of test cricket in front of him if he wants it. He is probably the only guy currently playing who has a chance of doing some damage to the Lara records.

Ajay Jadeja is a neat little guy who can really hammer it when he gets going. The fact that he is a prince probably takes some of the acid off in terms of making a living, but he loves playing at the highest level and demonstrates real enjoyment every time he plays. He was kind enough to organise a trip to a carpet maker in Delhi for us, a gesture which is certainly outside the norm and one which very few players would do.

To hone the art of swing bowling in Indian conditions is an outstanding achievement and Kapil Dev has certainly had to work for his world record. I didn't play him until later in his career and he'd slowed down a lot, and I found his approach a wee bit superior. It was really the way he just ambled from slip to slip as if to say "I'm a cricket legend, who the hell are you?" which got me.

Playing for a World XI at Scarborough in the final game of the Indians' 1990 tour of England, I made a hundred in the first innings and was on my way to another. Kapil came over and started remonstrating with me. "Greatbatch, you must get out – you cannot get two hundreds in this game, it is a festival game." On and on he went, but to me it was a first class game and I wasn't going to hit one up in the air just because he was a bit bored.

One of the more likeable guys in the Indian side was Ravi Shastri. Ravi is very anglicised from all his time in county cricket and made sure we were well looked after during the 1995 tour. Strangely, he always seemed to get stick from his own crowd, because he would have made most sides in the world when at his peak.

Life after cricket has been good for him and he manages a company called Champions which has Sachin Tendulkar on its books – he wouldn't need too many other clients to make a dollar. Had I made the 1995 World Cup, Ravi had a sponsor for my bats and equipment who was prepared to pay £15,000 for the period of the tournament alone! It's not just the honour of representing your country that you miss out on at times.

The mistake that people make in not getting to know their opposition was brought home to me last year. We had always found Manoj Prabhakar hard work and no-one in the side really liked him, but during the rained out series in 1995 we were staying at the same hotel as the Indians and I managed to strike up a conversation. I saw a completely different side to him and he was very pleasant company. The only thing I haven't managed to get from him is the secret behind his quicker one arriving about two yards sooner!

Not many cricketers would have Pakistanis in their friends chapter, but playing in England has allowed me to meet a few of them away from the pressures of test cricket. The thing we have to understand about the Pakistan team is their desperation to win, based largely on the fact that the alternative for them is pretty unattractive. If you're not at the right end of the caste system, being dropped from the Pakistan team can mean a pretty bleak future.

Javed Miandad was plucked from the wrong side of the tracks and has become a national hero. There's no doubt he's a bugger to play against because he's so competitive, but off the track he is a lovely guy and looked after us wonderfully in 1990. Anyone who can take the piss out of the opposition while batting and get away with it has certainly got something special.

Mudassar Nazar is virtually an Englishman now and used to love touring New Zealand. Much of the attraction was cold Steinlager, which he'd give a bit of a nudge on tour. I played plenty of cricket with him in England and his little swingers would nick even the best players out. He's a very sincere and jovial character and it was always a pleasure to walk into a benefit game dressing room and see "Mud" sitting in the corner.

In stark contrast is Imran Khan – one of the most arrogant men I've ever met. Hogan and I once played in a charity match in England organised by David Frost. Imran was playing in our side and when we greeted him he looked at us and then just turned away; unbelievable behaviour. After Pakistan won the World Cup, hearing him proclaiming it as "my World Cup" was pretty hard to take. Winning that semi would have been great just for the pleasure of stuffing it up him. Imran pioneered reverse swing but is so arrogant he doesn't even consider it cheating.

I've mentioned the two "Ws" elsewhere in the book but they are certainly among my most respected opponents. When we first started playing each other it was a real "hate-hate" situation but before the last tour our relationship improved a bit. Both teams were at a function and because I felt the antics from both sides had got a bit silly I went over and had a yarn with the quick men. (Besides, I thought I might have been opening!) Both guys agreed that things had become a little strong and we have got on better ever since, although that doesn't diminish the intensity on the field.

The South Africans have eased back into test cricket comfortably and like their rugby players are hard men who do not enjoy losing. I shared the twelfth man duties with Pat Symcox during the centenary test and thought he was a super bloke. Pat's played a lot of first class cricket and had resigned himself to probably never playing for his country because of the sporting bans. Now that he is involved I think he sees it as a real bonus and loves playing for South Africa, but he also makes the most of being in whatever country he is in.

When Marina and Alice (who was very new to the world) were sitting uncomfortably at Eden Park, Pat was good enough to take them into the viewing area and make them comfortable, which was a lovely gesture and demonstrated his gentlemanly side.

Another gentlemanly South African is Hansie Cronje who has become one of the better batsmen in the world in terms of adaptability to one-day and test cricket. Much of this development must go down to his training which he is absolutely fanatical about – I watched he and Kepler Wessels throw ball after ball at each other one morning, working really hard at perfecting little aspects of their game.

For me, though, the man who epitomises South African cricket is Clive Rice. Clive was an incredibly strong man who was very quick before his back gave way and he and Richard Hadlee at Notts must have been a nightmare for opposition teams. It was a real privilege to play alongside him during Hadlee's benefit season and it was clear in the way he played he was one of the top cricketers in the world, sadly robbed of international competition. I always felt he had an aura about him, and now that he is in charge of the South African cricket academy, we can expect some talented and tough-minded South Africans to represent their country in years to come.

The Sri Lankans are a lovely group of people and have some magnificent players in their line-up. Asanka Gurasinha is one who has enjoyed a heap of success against us and for that reason loves visiting New Zealand. I think the social life suits him pretty well also and he is great company.

During the bomb saga he was good enough to come to the hotel and talk to me about the situation and what we might expect in the future. Although he was keen for the tour to proceed he said there was no guarantee about safety, for although we were unlikely to be targeted we could be in the wrong place at the wrong time. It was good to talk to someone I could trust who was very up front about the issues.

A guy making 260 when you've dropped him on ninety is fair enough reason to keep him out of your life story. When the batsman is Aravinda Da Silva, exceptions can be made. Aravinda is a super bloke; a humble, quiet man, rated by the quicks as one of the very best hookers and cutters in the game.

My experience with grassing him came at the Basin. When Willie bowled him a short one (not a good idea, Will), Aravinda just went boof toward me about twenty metres away at square leg – it was fairground attraction time again as this red bullet came fizzing toward me and I was lucky to even tip it over the bar. While the boys bowled shorter and shorter, he just hit harder and harder – he seemed to pick it up so quickly.

Arjuna "the Chef" Ranatunga is a competitive and successful player. Seldom does he miss out on getting a start and he often goes on with it. Ranatunga has played for many years and has been integral in turning Sri Lanka from just another nation into one of the most competitive – their test record is ever improving and their one-day status speaks for itself. Although he visits the same dietitian as Inzamam, there is no denying his contribution to the growth and development of Sri Lankan cricket. In a team of nice guys he adds the competitive steel and at times can be quite abrasive – ask Kerry Walmsley!

I haven't had the experience of playing test cricket against the Windies but through my England experiences have had numerous opportunities to pit my skills against them and to line up with them, an infinitely more comfortable experience.

Richie Richardson was a real Joe Cool even to the point of donning his shades in the bar after the game. You don't need their protection out in the middle in most English summers, but Rich would always have them firmly attached. He might have seemed perfectly relaxed at all times, but he was ultra-competitive and must have been distressed by his poor run of form over the last couple of years.

I met Brian Lara when he was just an emerging talent, having not played a great deal of first class stuff, let alone test matches. I was living with my agent, John Farrar, when Lara phoned from the airport wondering where his car was. He must have thought the world would fall at his feet – he was subsequently proved right – and he certainly had expectations beyond his record early on. Probably more than anything, it demonstrated the self-belief and arrogance that only the very best seem to have.

One guy who took self-belief and arrogance to new heights was Gordon Greenidge. I had watched from the stand with admiration the way he had played Richard Hadlee on the way to a double hundred at Eden Park in 1987. It was very green and his judgement and shot execution was extra special. When I learnt he was joining us for an exhibition game I was excited about meeting him and looking forward to a chat.

Gordon was nowhere to be seen when the game started and arrived after the batting order had been organised. After he turned up he asked what the order was (he was down the list a bit) and then went and put his pads on, which I thought a little odd. Richie Richardson was smashing it out in the middle and I was next in, looking forward to batting with one of the game's greats. Richardson was on eighty when the next wicket fell and as I rose to join him Greenidge just pushed past with a curt "I'm going out now." I couldn't believe it.

There must have been some sort of rivalry going on because Greenidge proceeded to absolutely murder it, to the extent that he made his hundred about ten minutes after Richie. The arrogance and plain bad manners stuck with me much more clearly than the innings, that's for sure.

Thankfully, the Windies have their share of good guys as well, none better than Otis Gibson. I was pleased to see Otis, a brilliant guy who really enjoys the game, making a name for himself in the 1995/96 World Series in Australia. I first caught up with him during a series of matches in South Africa, where a World XI had assembled to play in a series for Kepler Wessels.

Otis is a bit of a rarity for the modern West Indies team in that he is an all-rounder, which they don't seem to produce these days. Otis had played a bit in South Africa and really felt at home but I was appalled when a Boer came up to me in a bar one night and said, "What are you doing with him?" It was a clear indication that not all South Africans had moved in their beliefs but Otis handled it with remarkable restraint. I'm sure he will be a very successful cricketer for the Windies.

The new kids on the block are the Zimbabwe boys. I had the experience of playing against them as a Young International and as a test player and it was good to see the consistency in their approach. Hard and competitive on the field, but keen on a beer and a bit of banter after the game.

Chicken farmer Eddo Brandes fits neatly into the big man, big thirst category and it is little wonder he has had fitness battles over the years. In a lot of ways he's worse than a Botham, always wanting to have fun, and he remained friendly even when the teams weren't on great terms in 1992. (Much of the animosity came from Hogan, but thankfully Eddo didn't seem too bothered.)

David Houghton has been Zimbabwean cricket for a decade or more and would have played in his fourth World Cup had he not broken his toe playing against us. During the Young International tour we would frequently have a bit of brekky at the ground before the start of play and he was a very generous host. He always batted in a very organised fashion and has played some great knocks for his country, particularly when they were getting started in tests.

One guy who used to hit it a long way for them was Ian Butchart. I had to go and fetch a few of his big hits in 1988 but by the time we returned in 1992 he had decided a couple of lagers on the sideline was a better bet, and he was putting a ton of pressure on the stitching of his shirt. Butch was a very competitive player and really enjoyed playing international cricket but like Eddo was a dangerous man to be around if he knew you were due a day off.

Those are a handful of the players who have graced the world stage while I've been around. Some I've played against dozens of times, some just once or twice, but all of them have had an impact on me in one way or another.

After playing for New Zealand, some of my best experiences in the game have been with many of these players on the charity fields of England. There is nothing like being in the same dressing room to break down barriers and really get to know the guys who weeks later will be running in trying to knock your block off. It is also great to watch the great batsmen of the world at close range, to talk to them, find out what makes them tick, and what little habits they might have that I could employ. I've been lucky to meet some wonderful people over my career and I'm glad I've been forward in getting to know them. There is so much more to sport than the games themselves, but you've got to go out and grab it.

Keep Moving Forward

I have no personal blueprint outlining how I would like New Zealand Cricket to be administered. Documents such as the Hood Report are the place for such recommendations and I'm happy to leave such things to the experts. I do have a few thoughts, though, on what we should be doing for our cricketers, not just at international level but first class players as well.

My thoughts coincide with many initiatives currently being undertaken by NZC and really are just a collection of ideas that I would like to see introduced over the next few years. They are largely, but not exclusively, for the younger guys, in order that they might play in an environment more in tune with their needs not only while they are playing but, crucially, when they are not.

Young players need to have a job – it's that simple. It is just not good enough to have talented young guys getting up late for a game of golf, going to the gym or watching videos. These guys need to be working in order that they understand about routines and disciplines and commitment to other people. As a young player I did exactly what I'm suggesting today's youngsters don't do and face my thirties looking to develop new skills. I've become a fish head* and I realise how demanding running an association is.

Roles in cricket administration are ideal for current players for there are a raft of learning opportunities available. Think about coaching skills, public-speaking skills, working within budgets, selling skills, marketing concepts and financial administration. Sure, a young Aucklander might be part of a bigger administration than a guy in Central Districts, but the principles are the same, and the learning opportunities just as great. The other benefit, of course, is the opportunity to understand more about the running of the sport they're in and give them a greater opportunity to achieve the balance between player needs and administrative capability.

The job search needn't be restricted to cricket administration and development. I know many companies would be delighted to have high calibre young people on their staff. Not just in a fuzzy "public appearance" type role, but working on projects to which they can make a genuine contribution within the boundaries of their cricket commitments.

Players should also be encouraged to seek tertiary qualifications during their career. Given the appropriate structure, a player might be able to complete a number of papers on an extramural basis and finish their careers with more than just a batting average to put on their CV.

I believe contracts are a move in the right direction, particularly with the emphasis on playing and winning. What they don't do is offer any great security and a player who is out of form and not selected has no other income to live on. A player with a mortgage and a family would have to play extremely well if he wanted to make a reasonable living out of cricket – a good concept perhaps, but lacking the surety that many would consider necessary.

It is unrealistic to expect figures such as the All Blacks

*administrator

command (which are probably distorted because of the competition for signatures) but if a player is expected to commit to being a full-time cricketer (in the absence of the job programme) the risk/reward ratio is a little skewed.

Players are making decisions to retire from first class cricket at a very young age. The recent De Groen/White survey discovered a staggeringly low number of players still involved at age 30. We are not talking about old age here and, disturbingly, we are talking about players who give the game away before they've reached their full potential.

Players in regular employment cannot use their leave entitlement to play cricket year after year, particularly when in many cases it is costing them money to compete. To pay guys sixty dollars a day expenses is laughable and although there is considerable expense involved in providing a reasonable remuneration for eighty-odd players, I believe it is a cost we have to bear.

There are those who argue first class cricket should fund itself and if the cricket was any good people would come and watch. This misses the fundamental reason for first class cricket – to provide a demanding level of cricket sufficient to prepare players for international competition. We must consider first class cricket as a development stage and an investment in our national side rather than a stand alone expense. This will not happen if first class cricket becomes effectively just another age group series, with most players in their mid-twenties.

Where are the Troups, the Cushens, the Franklins and others like them who would provide a real test for young players coming through. Having the old hands gives an excellent point of reference to a selector when assessing players' performances one-on-one in a match situation.

On a similar theme, I believe we need to work harder in terms of developing an appropriate apprenticeship for players before they are selected for New Zealand. Too often, players are selected the moment they hit a couple off the square or bowl a side out on a sub-standard result wicket. The number of players selected in the 'nineties indicates quite clearly that the selectors haven't been sure whether or not a player has the mental capabilities to succeed at the top level.

One of the obvious criteria is a track record. Players here are selected having scored one or two hundreds at first class level; players in Australia have usually got into double figures in terms of hundreds scored before they even get a look in. Where and how players are scoring their runs is critical also, for we need to know whether the attack was a little above club level on a flat one or did the runs come on a tricky wicket against a strong attack.

Stephen Fleming's quest for that maiden test hundred has been well documented and I'm sure he will score the first of many very soon. It is pure speculation but would he have been able to pick up the test hundred habit earlier with more hundreds and more disciplines behind him at first class level? We'll never know, of course, but the point is that players will benefit more from a structured path to the top rather than being rushed in and not reaching their potential.

Coaching plays a big part in the way we play the game and I believe it is an area we must look hard at in terms of emphasis rather than expertise. While technique is important and must never be underplayed, I believe there is a danger in stifling players' personalities if we get too hung up on technique. A look at a dozen top golfers' swings would reveal similar fundamentals but differing styles in terms of execution; a similar philosophy with our young players may see them express their ability far more freely. The last thing we want is all our youngsters batting like Geoffrey Boycott.

The role of wives and families needs close attention. My thinking is based on the simple premise that if the family needs are being taken care of in terms of seats and facilities for children, players have one less thing to thinking about and the partners can come and support knowing they will be looked after. In Australia, Castlemaine, the sponsors of the Australian team, provide a room for the players' wives where they can attend to babies' needs and other such necessities. Lunch is provided and the women feel as if they are part of the picture. The Australian wives have looked after their New Zealand counterparts splendidly, and it can be embarrassing when attempting to return the hospitality.

The example of the Auckland rugby team, which included partners and even parents, is clear indication of how consideration for players' families actually strengthens the whole unit. It is also a good example of how such an approach does not cloud the clear boundaries between immediate team responsibilities and the wider support network.

The Bank of New Zealand have begun to lead the way in terms of appreciating the contribution of partners. On one occasion they flew the women to Wellington and we went up Mt Victoria on a bus for a champagne function. On arrival we noticed a guy a little bit further up the hill who was clearly hammered and looked like a real down and outer. When he got up as if to come and talk to us he fell over and rolled down the hill, but then proceeded to come over and talk to some of the partners.

We were horrified until we realised it was comedian Mark Wright, who proceeded to entertain us for the rest of the evening. It was a great night and a great gesture from the bank.

Naturally, these things will take some time to put in place and some may well not be acted upon. I consider the job situation to be number one in terms of priority – let's equip our young players with the skills they'll need after the game while giving them the time they need to train and become outstanding performers at test level. It is a balance that can be achieved with careful management and one any player with sense will welcome.

There is nothing surer than cricket not being able to provide sufficient income for a player to retire on, and there is a long time between the boots going in the cupboard and the rest home.

The Cricket Academy is definitely moving things in the right direction but we must remember that not every cricketer will take that path. Yes, we need to provide special facilities for our elite youngsters but not all of them will graduate and we need to recognise a wider group of players.

It is important to consider all ideas from those within the game as well as those from other sports and business environments. Provided the suggestions and criticisms are designed to keep advancing the game then all should be given due consideration. It is encouraging that the current administration is moving forward and making every effort to make the game better for every stakeholder.

I have been lucky to have had a good run with the New Zealand side and have been very proud to have represented my country. I guess the only thing I would change would be my batting average, for what a great way it has been to spend the past ten or fifteen years of my life.

Form and fitness allowing, I would like to help take New Zealand back to competitiveness – we have the players and with the right environment can achieve good results in both forms of the game. I hope the New Zealand public will continue to support the team – to be demanding but recognise that no team wins all its matches. As my profession should, let's create an environment where everyone is enjoying their involvement . . . being challenged, learning, but finding real satisfaction in being part of the game of cricket.

STATISTICS

to end of 1995/96 season

Compiled by Francis Payne

First Class

	Batting									Bowling			
Season	*M*	*I*	*NO*	*HS*	*Runs*	*Ave*	*100*	*50*	*ct*	*Wkts*	*Runs*	*Ave*	*Best*
1982/83	4	8	0	80	205	25.63	–	1	–				
1983/84	8	14	2	39	129	10.75	–	–	5				
1984/85	5	8	1	67	234	33.42	–	2	2				
1985/86	7	12	4	119*	316	39.50	1	1	9	0	2	–	–
1986/87	9	17	2	135	681	45.40	3	1	7				
1987/88	10	19	1	149	795	44.16	2	4	10				
1988 (E)	1	2	1	26*	32	32.00	–	–	1				
1988/89 (Z)	3	5	0	81	156	31.20	–	1	4				
1988/89 (I)	6	10	1	90*	270	30.00	–	2	4				
1988/89	7	13	2	202*	562	51.09	1	4	9	0	6	–	–
1989/90 (A)	3	5	1	146*	261	65.25	1	1	3				
1989/90	10	15	1	86	408	29.14	–	2	8	0	0	–	–
1990 (E)	11	16	3	168*	744	57.23	2	4	7				
1990/91 (P)	5	9	1	102*	251	31.37	1	–	2				
1990/91	4	8	2	102*	319	53.16	1	2	8				
1991/92	10	17	0	81	366	21.52	–	2	12	0	57	–	–
1992 (E)	1	1	0	45	45	45.00	–	–	1				
1992/93 (Z)	3	6	1	126*	392	78.40	1	3	2				
1992/93	8	15	0	133	372	24.80	1	1	7				
1993/94 (A)	5	9	0	65	216	24.00	–	2	2				
1993/94	5	10	2	65*	259	32.37	–	2	3				
1994 (E)	9	18	3	84	528	35.20	–	3	4				
1994/95	7	11	0	131	526	47.82	2	1	6	1	23	23.00	1-23
1995/96 (I)	6	8	0	138	387	48.37	2	1	5				
1995/96	5	6	2	202	623	155.75	4	–	9	0	30	–	–
TOTAL	**152**	**262**	**30**	**202***	**9077**	**39.12**	**22**	**40**	**130**	**1**	**118**	**118.00**	**1-23**

Record For Each Team

For	*M*	*I*	*NO*	*HS*	*Runs*	*Ave*	*100*	*50*	*ct*	*Wkts*	*Runs*	*Ave*	*Best*
Auckland	24	42	7	119*	884	25.25	1	4	16	0	2	–	–
Central Dist	50	89	7	202*	3737	45.57	12	13	60	1	116	116.00	1-23
NZ (tests)	39	67	5	146*	1981	31.95	3	10	27	0	0	–	–
NZ (other)	28	46	6	126*	1724	43.10	4	10	16				
Others	11	18	5	168*	751	57.76	2	3	11				
TOTAL	**152**	**262**	**30**	**202***	**9077**	**39.12**	**22**	**40**	**130**	**1**	**118**	**118.00**	**1-23**

Centuries

119*	Auckland v Central Districts	Auckland	1985/86
117*	Central Districts v Wellington	Levin	1986/87
135	Central Districts v Northern Districts	Morrinsville	1986/87
126	Central Districts v Canterbury	New Plymouth	1986/87
149	Central Districts v Canterbury	Blenheim	1987/88
107*	New Zealand v England	Auckland	1987/88
202*	Central Districts v Otago	Palmerston North	1988/89
146*	New Zealand v Australia	Perth	1989/90
168*	World XI v India[1]	Scarborough	1990
128*	World XI v India[2]	Scarborough	1990
102*	New Zealand v PIA	Rawalpindi	1990/91
102*	Central Districts v Canterbury	Christchurch	1990/91
126*	New Zealand v Zimbabwe B	Harare	1992/93
133	New Zealand v Pakistan	Hamilton	1992/93
131	Central Districts v Wellington	Napier	1994/95
125	Central Districts v Northern Districts	New Plymouth	1994/95
138	New Zealand v President's XI	Rajkot	1995/96
100	New Zealand v Bombay	Bombay	1995/96
115	Central Districts v Canterbury	Christchurch	1995/96
202	Central Districts v Northern Districts	Rotorua	1995/96
162*	Central Districts v Auckland	Auckland	1995/96
126*	Central Districts v Otago	Napier	1995/96

[1]First innings [2]second innings

Shell Cup

Season	*M*	*I*	*NO*	*HS*	*Runs*	*Ave*	*S/R*	*100*	*50*	*ct*
1982/83	1	1	0	7	7	7.00	29	–	–	1
1983/84	4	3	0	75	154	51.33	50	–	1	1
1984/85	2	2	0	15	26	13.00	54	–	–	2
1985/86	2	2	0	8	15	7.50	83	–	–	–
1986/87	5	5	0	43	94	18.80	47	–	–	2
1987/88	5	5	0	67	192	38.40	64	–	1	1
1989/90	5	5	3	80*	246	123.00	65	–	3	1
1990/91	3	3	0	55	55	18.33	54	–	1	2
1991/92	5	5	1	78*	123	30.75	56	–	1	4
1993/94	7	7	0	69	261	37.28	72	–	2	9
1994/95	3	3	0	51	77	25.66	90	–	1	2
1995/96	7	7	0	84	172	24.57	55	–	1	5
TOTAL	**49**	**48**	**4**	**84**	**1422**	**32.31**	**61**	**–**	**11**	**30**

Tests

Season	*v*	*M*	*I*	*NO*	*HS*	*Runs*	*Ave*	*100*	*50*	*ct*
1987/88	E	2	3	1	107*	186	93.00	1	1	–
1988/89	I	3	6	1	90*	196	39.20	–	1	3
1988/89	P	1	2	1	76	89	89.00	–	1	–
1989/90	A	1	2	1	146*	222	222.00	1	1	1
1989/90	I	3	3	0	46	93	31.00	–	–	–
1989/90	A	1	1	0	16	16	16.00	–	–	1
1990	E	3	4	0	47	115	28.75	–	–	–
1990/91	P	3	6	0	43	89	14.83	–	–	2
1990/91	SL	2	4	1	65	99	33.00	–	1	5
1991/92	E	1	2	0	11	11	5.50	–	–	2
1992/93	Z	2	4	0	88	243	60.75	–	3	2
1992/93	P	1	2	0	133	141	70.50	1	–	2
1992/93	A	3	6	0	61	126	21.00	–	1	3
1993/94	A	3	6	0	35	67	11.16	–	–	1
1993/94	P	3	6	0	48	105	17.50	–	–	3
1993/94	I	1	2	0	27	39	19.50	–	–	–
1994	E	1	2	0	21	21	10.50	–	–	–
1994/95	SL	2	3	0	46	47	15.66	–	–	–
1995/96	I	3	3	0	50	76	25.33	–	1	2
TOTAL		**39**	**67**	**5**	**146***	**1981**	**31.95**	**3**	**10**	**27**

Test Batting Record Against Each Country

Against	*M*	*I*	*NO*	*HS*	*Runs*	*Ave*	*100*	*50*
Australia	8	15	1	146*	431	30.78	1	2
England	7	11	1	107*	333	33.30	1	1
India	10	14	1	90*	404	31.07	–	2
Pakistan	8	16	1	133	424	28.26	1	1
Sri Lanka	4	7	1	65	146	24.33	–	1
Zimbabwe	2	4	0	88	243	60.75	–	3
TOTAL	**39**	**67**	**5**	**146***	**1981**	**31.95**	**3**	**10**

Batting Record as Opener and Non-Opener

	M	*I*	*NO*	*HS*	*Runs*	*Ave*	*100*	*50*
Opener	11	21	0	133	637	30.33	1	5
Non-Opener	28	46	5	146*	1344	32.78	2	5
TOTAL	**39**	**67**	**5**	**146***	**1981**	**31.95**	**3**	**10**

One-Day Internationals

Season	*v*	*M*	*I*	*NO*	*HS*	*Runs*	*Ave*	*S/R*	*100*	*50*	*ct*
1987/88	E	4	4	1	64*	112	37.33	67	–	1	1
1987/88	SC	4	4	0	47	119	29.75	74	–	–	2
1988/89	I	4	4	1	84*	149	49.66	89	–	2	1
1988/89	P	4	4	1	35*	51	17.00	82	–	–	1
1989/90	Tri	5	5	0	53	77	15.40	58	–	1	1
1989/90	AAC	3	3	0	37	73	24.33	54	–	–	–
1990	E	2	2	1	111	213	213.00	89	2	–	–
1990/91	P	3	3	0	36	44	14.66	75	–	–	–
1990/91	WS	3	3	0	20	46	15.33	76	–	–	1
1990/91	SL	3	3	1	29*	69	34.50	73	–	–	–
1990/91	E	2	2	0	12	12	6.00	37	–	–	–
1991/92	E	3	3	0	10	19	6.33	44	–	–	4
1991/92	WC	7	7	0	73	313	44.71	87	–	3	4
1992/93	Z	2	2	0	55	76	38.00	104	–	1	2
1992/93	P	3	3	0	24	31	10.33	41	–	–	1
1992/93	A	5	5	0	68	121	24.20	53	–	1	3
1993/94	WS	7	7	0	50	177	25.29	64	–	1	2
1993/94	P	3	3	0	23	46	15.33	54	–	–	2
1993/94	NZC	4	4	0	76	190	47.50	76	–	2	3
1994/95	SL	2	2	0	43	60	30.00	75	–	–	2
1995/96	I	5	5	0	38	88	17.60	65	–	–	2
TOTAL		**78**	**78**	**5**	**111**	**2086**	**28.57**	**72**	**2**	**12**	**32**

Key: *Tri – Triangular Tournament; AAC – Austral-Asia Cup; WC – World Cup; SC – Sharjah Cup; WS – World Series; NZC – New Zealand Centenary.*

One-Day Batting Record Against Each Country

Against	*M*	*I*	*NO*	*HS*	*Runs*	*Ave*	*SR*	*100*	*50*
Australia	17	17	0	74	410	24.11	69	–	3
Bangladesh	1	1	1	32	32	32.00	76	–	–
England	13	13	2	111	410	37.27	80	2	1
India	15	15	1	84*	500	35.71	78	–	4
Pakistan	16	16	1	35*	235	15.66	61	–	–
South Africa	5	5	0	76	189	37.80	83	–	2
Sri Lanka	7	7	1	43	156	26.00	76	–	–
West Indies	1	1	0	63	63	63.00	81	–	1
Zimbabwe	3	3	0	55	91	30.33	102	–	1
TOTAL	**78**	**78**	**5**	**111**	**2086**	**28.57**	**72**	**2**	**12**